MY FIRST YEAR AS A LAWYER

REAL-WORLD STORIES FROM AMERICA'S LAWYERS

Edited by
Mark Simenhoff

A SIGNET BOOK

SIGNET
Published by the Penguin Group
Penguin Books USA Inc., 375 Hudson Street,
New York, New York 10014, U.S.A.
Penguin Books Ltd, 27 Wrights Lane,
London W8 5TZ, England
Penguin Books Australia Ltd, Ringwood,
Victoria, Australia
Penguin Books Canada Ltd, 10 Alcorn Avenue,
Toronto, Ontario, Canada M4V 3B2
Penguin Books (N.Z.) Ltd, 182–190 Wairau Road,
Auckland 10, New Zealand

Penguin Books Ltd, Registered Offices:
Harmondsworth, Middlesex, England

Published by Signet, an imprint of Dutton Signet,
a division of Penguin Books USA Inc.
This is an authorized reprint of an edition published by Walker and Company. For information address Walker Publishing Company, Inc., 435 Hudson Street, New York, New York 10014.

First Signet Printing, September, 1996
10 9 8 7 6 5 4 3 2 1

Printed in the United States of America

Contents

Foreword

I grew up in the 1960s watching Perry Mason on television. For me, Perry Mason personified the essence of a lawyer. He had a razor-sharp mind and dark eyes that could see right through a lying witness. His presence was so commanding, and his questioning so incisive, that week after week mere spectators in the courtroom would jump up and blurt out that they were actually the guilty party. Perry Mason was so skilled that everybody felt a compulsion to confess—the bailiff, the jury, even the judge. Strangers off the street would burst into the courtroom and admit to the crime.

Perry Mason was a hero, defending innocent people against the government's wrongful accusations. To the best of my memory, he never once represented a guilty person. Of course, I eventually learned that Perry Mason's portrayal of a lawyer was not very realistic. Given the show's simplistic premise, it's perhaps fitting that the program was broadcast in black and white.

The 1980s offered up "L.A. Law." The glitzy

television show provided no greater insight into the daily lives of most lawyers than did Perry Mason. Law practice was depicted as revolving almost completely around money, sex, power, egos, and personality conflicts—as if the entire cast of "The Young and the Restless" had gone out and earned law degrees. Television entertainment is just that; it rarely lets accuracy get in the way of a scintillating story.

So what's it really like to practice law? How do you know if you should become a lawyer? As a law professor, I encounter law students still struggling with these questions. As they learn about the profession, some find it exciting and challenging; others decide it's not for them and drop out or decide to pursue other careers after graduating. Almost all would have benefited from better information about lawyering before deciding to attend law school.

What do lawyers do all day? First, they read a lot. Young lawyers especially spend a great deal of time researching in the library or, increasingly, on a computer. Second, lawyers write a lot. They draft memoranda, briefs, letters, contracts, and many other documents. The writing must be careful and precise; in many respects the law is an exacting, technical, and highly analytical field.

Lawyers also spend time interacting with other people. They give advice to clients, interview witnesses, and negotiate and meet with other lawyers. Some lawyers even go to court(!).

The law degree offers opportunities to work in virtually any area that might interest you, whether it be government, business, technology, civil rights, the environment, entertainment, international relations—any field. All areas of human activity involve legal issues that need to be addressed.

Lawyers work in many different settings. Law firms range in size from individual practitioners to firms with more than a thousand lawyers and offices scattered around the world. Lawyers work for the government, corporate in-house legal departments, legal clinics for low-income clients, and the military. A few (mostly people, like myself, with personality defects) decide to become law professors.

Good lawyering is hard work. It requires commitment and responsibility. "L.A. Law" notwithstanding, very little of law practice is glamorous. Lawyers frequently are under a great deal of pressure because people's rights and often the course of their lives depend on how well their lawyer performs. Being a lawyer isn't a nine-to-five job either; clients' legal needs can rarely be scheduled conveniently into an eight-hour day.

Law demands not only an intense commitment of time but also compassion and sound judgment. The practice of law often places the lawyer in the middle of difficult, and even bitter, conflicts between people. Lawyers have to be able to be firm but fair and deal with emotionally draining situations in a professional manner. As in any field of work, in the first year of law practice the learning curve is very steep, and dealing with these issues for the first time can be challenging and exhausting.

Lawyering can also be exciting and satisfying work. It's rewarding to serve people who need your help, to solve legal problems honestly and ethically, and to help resolve disputes. Lawyering involves critical reasoning, intellectual challenges, learning about new subjects, and meeting interesting people. A legal career can provide learning opportunities throughout one's life. Legal training also offers a way to give public service through civic involvement and pro bono work.

It is important to choose a career for the right reasons. Although a legal career can offer a comfortable living and a degree of status, these considerations by themselves are generally unwise reasons to choose the law as a career. You need to find out whether you would enjoy being a lawyer. Life is much too precious and short to spend your days working at a job you hate. On the other hand, working in a career that you truly love can be deeply and personally fulfilling. This book is designed to give you a taste of some of the challenges and rewards of the first year of practicing law. If the stories in this book engage and intrigue you in a personal way, I urge you to give serious thought to a career in the law.

—James D. Gordon III,
professor of law,
Brigham Young University

WHAT THEY NEVER SHOWED YOU ON *PERRY MASON* . . .

Draw back the curtain of glamour and take a close look at all the tension, conflict, drudgery—and satisfaction—of taking on a law practice. Accounts like the following will help you decide whether or not a career as an attorney is for you:

- Virginia Martinez returned to her community to help new Hispanic citizens with the intricacies of the law—and discovered the burdens inherent in being a Latina lawyer.
- Suzanne Boxer became a clerk writing the draft opinion for parents who wanted to prevent their child from receiving medical care that was against their religious beliefs—and learned how intimately the law could become involved in people's lives.
- Gregory D. Winfree leapt at the opportunity of working on a high-profile corporate case with one of his firm's most revered partners—and realized he was going to carry the whole case virtually on his own.
- Noreen Marcus fulfilled her father's lifelong dream of receiving a law degree—and found out that the best way of putting it to use was *not* becoming a lawyer.
- And more . . .

Acknowledgments

My thanks go first to the contributors for sharing the heretofore private memories that this volume comprises. These harried lawyers all took time out of their busy professional and family schedules, always at night or on weekends, to meet strict deadlines and suffer my badgering and silly questions.

My gratitude also goes to Brenda, Vidya, Janet, and Jeff, for proofreading and critiquing various portions of the drafts. Ceil—thanks for typing every page so promptly. Steve—thanks for sharing your computer expertise. You both spared me a thousand headaches.

Without the faith of two Marys in me, I would not have had the opportunity to work on this book. Mary Thompson, a former colleague who knew little more about me than what she'd heard in an oral rendition of my résumé, passed my name along to another Mary. Mary Kennan Herbert, the recipient of a single phone call, a batch of my newspaper clips, and a hastily prepared proposal, gave me a chance. To both Marys I am grateful.

Introduction

If you're thinking of becoming a lawyer or just want to learn more about what beginning lawyers do, welcome to this book.

As the true stories here vividly demonstrate, lawyers aren't born knowing how to practice their craft; they develop their skills through a mix of intensive schooling and practical on-the-job experience. Law school alone cannot turn a law student into a lawyer; thousands of students who graduate each year from law school have been fed heaping portions of theory but often receive almost no hands-on instruction on how to practice law or insight into what it means to be a lawyer. There are few law school courses that teach a neophyte lawyer where to locate the right statute book, how to present a case to a jury, or deal with a difficult client. These things lawyers learn and perfect only on the job. Once a student finishes law school and passes the bar exam, the real education begins: the process of becoming a lawyer.

This book contains stories by and about real

lawyers—all recalling their first year of practice—sharing the thorny episodes and dilemmas they faced during their first year of practice. Although their stories revolve around their roles as lawyers, the lessons they learned are relevant to much of life outside the courtroom, in all spheres of life. The contributors to this volume write of dealing with death or with a difficult boss. Others recount developing an enriching experience with a mentor, making friends, or keeping one's cool under frustrating circumstances. At the center of most of the stories is a story about responsibility—delivering for a client—in the midst of trying circumstances. The stories also touch on the tensions, needs, and contradictions that pull us every which way in a crisis in any profession.

As the contributors found out without exception, abstract legal theories are of little use to the beginning lawyer who can't adapt to the uncertainties that arise in everyday legal practice. Like all beginners, neophyte lawyers often learn their lessons by losing face—or at least thinking they have.

As the lawyers found, the experience usually is worth it, for from missteps and hard knocks emerges a more confident and capable attorney. Most of the writers convey an immediate sense of accomplishment, a feeling that future challenges won't be as daunting. Often the lessons are immediately apparent. Other times, the significance of a case takes years to imprint itself on the lawyer's consciousness.

Practicing law is an inherently confrontational activity, with winners and losers. Lawyers always seem to be "doing battle" with an opponent. As told in "Law and the Latina," Virginia Martinez remembers being acutely aware of the tension between winning her client's case and at the same time sympathizing with the predicament in which her legal "victory" places her client's opponent. Justice is a slippery concept at best and, Martinez implies, one party's courtroom success may do little to further society's best interests. "I was happy that I had 'won' the case and was gratified by the good wishes of more senior colleagues. But I knew the legal victory was of limited usefulness. While I had bought Sylvia time to avoid her family's ending up on the streets, no one's problems were really solved. My client still had no job, no husband—and ten children."

In winning her case, Martinez also realizes she wasn't necessarily fulfilling her motivation for going to law school, to help the poor community she grew up in.

In contrast, Randa Zagzoug reveals in "The Right Reason for Going to Law School" that her motivation for deciding to study law was nowhere near as idealistic as Martinez's. "Unlike those who went to law school because they liked the courtroom theatrics of litigation or the prospect of making a lot of money, I went for another reason: I was shy."

Searching during her three years in law school for a satisfying way to use her legal training, Zagzoug found herself drawn to immigration law. Her reaction to an interview with a Haitian asylum seeker came to symbolize for her both a cause and justification for the work she does today.

Like all professionals who provide a service, lawyers are under immense pressure to perform well for their clients. And people who pay their fees expect results, sometimes on very short notice and with exquisite attention to detail under exhausting circumstances. Corporate lawyers in top law markets like New York, Los Angeles, and Washington, D.C., typify practitioners in the business professionals' version of a college "all-nighter." These students often are the top finishers in their classes at the nation's top law schools and get paid handsomely to put in the grueling, intensive hours that would make most of us pull our hair out. In "The Glamour of Corporate Law—Sleeping on the Floor," Robert Zochowski describes his professional baptism by fire as a corporate lawyer. Zochowski's chronology of a particularly draining three-day legal marathon shows just how unglamorous the reality of corporate law can be. No one is fatigue-immune, but the time commitment required of the high-stakes corporate lawyer, Zochowski writes, is unique. "Some call this method 'sink or swim.' It isn't easy, and it isn't kind to those who sink, but in many ways there simply is no other way to gain the experience necessary to mature as a large-firm corporate lawyer."

Big responsibility isn't the exclusive province of the corporate lawyer. All lawyers, to a greater or lesser degree, feel this. In "Justice for a Guilty Country Boy," Sue Kessler tells that long hours aren't the only thing that keeps lawyers up at night. There also is a burden of being responsible for another human being's destiny, in Kessler's case a young kid named Brian. "We were both nervous as hell, Brian because he was facing jail time and a criminal record, and I, because I had his life in my hands—and it didn't seem there was much I could do for him."

In fact, it turned out there was something Kessler could do for her first felony client, and the tale of how she extricated him from a certain conviction exemplifies one lawyer's ability to adapt.

In law school, lawyers are trained to focus on highly theoretical, narrow issues—not the best course regimen for a young person trying to get a handle on the "big picture." Like Kessler, David Dominguez didn't think there was much he could do for his client, a union member who felt he was wrongly passed over for a plum job. In "A Lesson in Justice," Dominguez learned how he sold his client—and himself—short, by failing to think beyond the immediate issue facing his client.

Dominguez's developing view of the law as a

vehicle for change is not necessarily the norm. Recourse to the law often comes after the underlying situation already is beyond salvaging. Personal injury lawyers, especially, seek money to compensate clients who have lost a loved one or have suffered serious injury. In "The Imperfection of Law and the Death of Lilly," Ji-Zhou Zhou's identification with the dead daughter of a family she was representing made it impossible for her to keep her emotions under wraps; at one point she cries with the family she is working for. "There was so little solace the law could provide a family that had lost its only hope in life."

The law's analytical and rational demands make it incompatible with tears and heartbreak, even when the lawyer is not directly involved with the parties in the case. Working as a judicial clerk, Suzanne Boxer found herself drafting an opinion for a judge and making the agonizing decision of whether to deny a dying child medical care: "A Case of Life and Death."

Being a lawyer needn't be so tormenting, as Laurie Levenson recounts in her paean to the federal judge who provided her with the priceless career advice that helped make her legal career so rewarding. In "The Judge Who Taught Me to Teach," Levenson recounts how her mentor's suggestion that she procure some real-world experience as a prosecutor before entering academia helped her shape her own career as a law professor. Levenson uses a souvenir of a case she prosecuted in the real world as a teaching "tool" of unforgettable impact in her classes today. "Every now and then in an evidence lecture, my students' attention will flag. I'll brandish the ax and tell the story of Punchy. My students are able to see that the law is alive."

Lessons applicable in the courtroom can come from outside the courtroom, too, as Merle Raph, a lawyer in rural Montana, finds out to his surprise—and a witness's disgust. In "Lambing and Lawyering," Ralph's apparent enlightenment came from helping a stricken sheep bear its offspring. The experience helped him recover his poise when he returned to question a witness whose examination he had flubbed before bringing the lambs into the world. "Sheep and cows generally do not lie or evade the truth as do self-serving witnesses."

Being a lawyer usually involves face-to-face contact with a client. Usually. As an appellate attorney for the indigent, Susan Emlet Crandall carried on her representation of Roger, a particularly fascinating client, through the post. In "The Inmate of Letters," Crandall reconstructs their correspondence to trace the development of her business relationship with Roger, a convict who becomes a sort of pen pal for Crandall, and later her friend. His opening written remark to Crandall was: "I have no confidence in legal aid." Later, after they met, he wrote, "I didn't know lawyers could cook." Crandall could cook a memorable meal for her friend. But she sadly discovers she can't concoct a recipe that will dissuade Roger from a life of crime.

Neil Kornfeld also gets a lesson in humility. In "The Cop, the 'Perp', and the Rookie Prosecutor," in which he shows up at his first trial with a strong case against the defendant, he isn't at all confident he can count on his key witness, a police officer. All the subpoenas and pretrial sworn testimony in the world, he realizes, won't win a conviction if the police officer doesn't do his job on the stand. Kornfeld learns that just as clients rely on their lawyers, so must lawyers depend on their witnesses. Kornfeld's story is also one of give-and-take. Just as prosecutors need cops as witnesses, so do police need the prosecutors to present the evidence they dig up. The relationship between the cop and prosecutor, tense as it can be, is necessary to the smooth functioning of the law-enforcement system. Kornfeld explains: "Often it's the little things that really matter. A prosecutor is eternally grateful to the police officer who takes the time to write up legible and intelligible reports. For the prosecutor, witnesses' phone numbers are a vital but often forgotten detail. Details can make or sink a case."

Marlon Primes found that good lawyering entails a delicate mixture of the social, the analytical, and the commonsensical. In "When Honey Is Better than Vinegar," Primes loses his temper during a deposition and then finds the witness clamming up when he resumes the questioning.

The successful lawyer, Primes says, must know how to tailor his individual approach—the lawyerly equivalent of the bedside manner—to different personalities.

In "Seaman Bartley Gets the Boot," Robert Visnick relates what to him is more than a job. Wanting to "live the adventure" of life in the armed forces, Visnick became a naval lawyer, or judge advocate. In the navy, Visnick quickly sees that military personnel aren't necessarily better behaved than their civilian counterparts and that what passes for a crime can differ, as well as the procedures used to prosecute transgressors. Visnick finds you can alter the decorum and the uniforms, but you can't change the effect law can have on people's lives. When people screw up in the military, it follows them for the rest of their days. Visnick does find the military system in some ways to be more forgiving than the civilian world. "There was a feeling that 'we're in this together'—even if I was prosecuting this guy."

Gregory D. Winfree didn't have that cozy feeling in "Out There on My Own," in which he tells of handling a somewhat complex case almost entirely by himself. Winfree's story seems nearly one of survival and confirms that some of the toughest experiences turn out to be the most valuable ones. Left to fend for himself, Winfree quickly comes to depend on himself. But in going it alone, Winfree resolves never to do so again. At a particularly difficult moment, Winfree finds comfort in learning that he isn't the first novice to get thrown to the wolves.

Finding oneself in an uncomfortable situation doesn't have to derail one's career, but it can indeed give one pause. In "My First Judicial Conference" William Dillof describes how he—a denizen of the suburbs—found himself in a judge's chambers with a cast of surreal characters he'd never forget. "Nothing prepared me for the bizarre, almost surreal lack of decorum that characterized this particular Bronx courtroom of the early 1970s."

Darien McWhirter's story, "Booty in the Law Library," describes another kind of boss, the kind who cares and takes the time to train and listen to his subordinates. Faced with a most improbable set of circumstances, McWhirter's "paternal" boss dissects an associate's mistake and shows him how to solve the sticky problem the mistake has caused.

Learning something new isn't confined to learning how to act in a given situation. It can involve thinking about the law in a new way. In "When Law Became More than Research," Monica Miller, a Washington, D.C., lawyer at the time, was forced to expand her conception of what practicing law meant. Faced with some research that had no answer, Miller discovered another side of the law as it's practiced, particularly in the nation's capital.

Practicing law isn't for everybody, as Noreen

Marcus discovers in the course of "Liberated from the Law." The death of her father helps her see herself more clearly and leads her to parlay her legal training into success in journalism, which she loved. Despite her decision to forsake a legal career, Marcus's story does attest to the positive experience of becoming a lawyer.

The decision not to practice law may be a lesson in disguise. For as the economy has weakened and businesses have begun reining in legal costs, the competition for jobs in the law has become extremely intense. Unlike the 1980s, a law school diploma is no longer a quick ticket to job security. A recent *Wall Street Journal* article suggested that the percentage of law school graduates in 1992 who were unemployed a half year after graduating is in the double digits. Since 1970, the number of lawyers in the United States has jumped 160 percent to 799,769 from 304,938, according to the American Bar Association. In that period, the population has risen by just over 20 percent.

Everyone, it seems, has a favorite joke or grouse about attorneys. Still, whom do people turn to when they've been wronged and need to settle the dispute without resorting to violence? A lawyer. As maligned as they are, lawyers are indispensable in our modern society, based as it is on the rule of law. Lawyers are the agents for the law. Lawyers keep criminals off the street and ensure that innocent people don't go to jail. They empower the powerless.

In short, lawyers are engaged in human activity in all its forms and all its nuances. In that sense it has become the most accessible of all the professions. One doesn't have to be enamored of numbers like an accountant or brave the rigors of chemistry, physics, and calculus as is generally required of doctors. As the tales in this book show, learning to be a lawyer often is little more than applying a little common sense.

1

Law and the Latina

Virginia Martinez

My client Sylvia was an immigrant from Mexico. She had no job, no husband, no money to pay her rent—and ten children depending on her to provide them with a roof over their heads. A judge was about to evict Sylvia's family unless I could pull a rabbit out of my legal top hat.

I had become a lawyer to try to change things in the poor, underprivileged Chicago community where I had lived most of my life. I had spent my last two years of law school working part-time for the legal services office two blocks from my home. Now I was working full-time for the office representing those who couldn't afford to hire a lawyer. In the rhetoric of the day, representing the poor in court was my way of "giving back to the community."

In eviction cases judges were usually strict in applying the law. The tenant either paid or got out. Luckily for Sylvia and for the case I was preparing—if not for the person affected—one of her children had ingested paint from the apartment walls, and traces of lead had been found in the child's blood. City officials were automatically alerted by the hospital, and an inspection of the block of old two-story buildings ensued.

The inspection gave me the legal ammunition I needed to try to pin a retaliatory eviction allegation against the landlord, an elderly Slavic woman who spoke not a word of English and who, like her troubled tenant, was having her own difficulties making ends meet. My strategy was to argue that Sylvia's family was being evicted in retribution for the investigation that had been initiated as a result of the lead poisoning.

Through her daughter the landlord complained on the witness stand about the misbehavior of my client's children and the fact that Sylvia continued to have babies even though she didn't have a husband and was living on public assistance.

Sylvia was a nervous witness. At one point she had difficulty remembering how many children she had.

The case bothered me, I didn't doubt the landlord's testimony, for I had seen Sylvia around the kids and had quickly gotten the feeling that she was not always able to control them. I had gone to law school to help people in need, and Sylvia needed help. But though I shared almost nothing culturally with the landlord, she, too, as far as I could tell, was trying to make her way in the world, just like Sylvia. The two beleaguered women had more in common than one might conclude at first glance. As a lawyer, however, I was bound to do my best for my client, and I did. Against the odds, I was trying to buy Sylvia the time she needed to find a new place for her brood to live and thrive. She and her family's dilemma were a highlight of my first year of practicing law.

The thought of going to law school had never entered my mind until I was in my senior year of college. When I finished college and began working as a secretary full-time, I began to do a lot of reading about social problems, and about the "Chicano movement."

While in college, I had been working part-time for two Hispanic attorneys who had a general practice in my neighborhood of Pilsen on the near West Side of Chicago. It was a community whose composition had changed from one of predominantly European immigrants to one containing mostly Mexican immigrants and first-generation Mexican-Americans. The neighborhood seemed to be adding poor immigrants to the mix at an even faster rate. Each year more children were on the streets during the summer.

I soon realized that I wanted to make a difference in my community and told my bosses I was considering getting a degree and going to graduate school to become a social worker. My bosses told me that I could do more for the community as a lawyer than as a social worker.

At the time, there were about fifteen Hispanic lawyers in all of Illinois! I could see from the cases that came in that there was definitely a need for more. More and more, as I took dictation from these two lawyers, I had the nagging feeling that I was "on the wrong side of the desk." I made up my mind: "If they can do it, I can do it." And I would do it. My parents and family weren't keen for me to attend law school. They thought having a basic college education was sufficient for success. To my mother, any white-collar job was a wonderful job. She was satisfied knowing that I didn't have to work in a factory. My father had decided when I graduated from high school that since I was probably going to get married, there was no need to invest in college tuition even if he had had enough money.

Women lawyers of any ethnic background weren't a common sight in the mid-1970s, so my being both Hispanic and female was a little too much for some people to understand. It was assumed that Latinas in the courtroom were either litigants or secretaries coming in to request continuances. Add to that the fact that I was twenty-five years old that first year, and you'll understand that I was a confusing presence to the judges, attorneys, and clerks I dealt with each day.

"Secretaries can't argue motions!" I was told when I checked in to argue one of my first cases in court. It was 1975, and I was one of the first two female Hispanic lawyers in Illinois. I informed the clerk that this particular secretary *was* an attorney. I received an apology, but I was indeed an anomaly.

Even my clients at the legal services office where I worked questioned whether I was really a lawyer. They assumed that since they were getting free legal services, they would probably not see a "real" attorney. For my clients, many of whom were immigrants from Mexico and spoke only Spanish, I was a source of pride. That I had managed to make it in a profession that had few minorities gave them a sense that our community was moving forward.

Like their clients, Hispanic lawyers had experiences I was quite sure differed from those of other lawyers, and somehow we were treated differently. Subtly, of course. Several times I was asked to translate for attorneys in other offices. I refused, saying, "I didn't go to law school to be an interpreter." Also, lawyers interested in trying to build class action cases or break legal ground often opted to hire translators rather than transfer such cases to bilingual lawyers such as myself. It seemed that the needs of the client in being able to speak directly with his or her attorney sometimes took a backseat to the intellectual interests or career ambitions of the attorney.

The cases that I did handle proved the need for Spanish-speaking attorneys. Many of my community's residents were defrauded in business transactions because they could not read English and did not understand the U.S. legal system. These were hardworking people who were just trying to take care of their families. There also were many unscrupulous car dealers, landlords, contractors, and real estate agents who saw the growing Hispanic population of Chicago as potential profit—an all-too-easy source of cash income.

There were, of course, many cases in which my clients were not contesting the position of the plaintiff but merely trying to work out payment arrangements or other ways of settling the controversy.

There were times when I intentionally set out to change people's perceptions of what attorneys should be like. Sometimes when I had a simple matter such as an agreed order or uncontested continuance, I would wear my waist-length hair in ponytails wrapped in suede strips. When people asked if I was "Indian," I would say, "Yes, my relatives were from northern Mexico. I am Native American, though not of a U.S. tribe." I was making a statement about my own culture but also forcing people to think about their stereotypes of attorneys. Diversity was entering the profession, and I wanted everyone to know it.

When I visited Sylvia and her family at home, I saw that the two- or three-bedroom apartment was entirely inadequate for a family of eleven. A window was cracked and had not been fixed. Sylvia told me that one of her children was responsible. It occurred to me that a landlord shouldn't be responsible for repairs like that and that my client had a duty to maintain her home, even a humble apartment.

Later, in the only court hearing I ever participated in with not one but two interpreters, the judge gave my client two months to look for a new apartment. When the landlady asked whether Sylvia would have to pay the rent until she moved, he said, "With ten kids, she's going to have a hard enough time finding an apartment, and she's going to need the money." My client had been issued a rare reprieve for a case like this, but I felt sorry for this landlord who would lose needed income as a result of the decision.

I was happy that I had won the case and was gratified by the good wishes of more senior colleagues. But I knew the legal victory was of limited usefulness. While I had bought Sylvia time to avoid her family's ending up on the streets, no one's problems were really solved. My client still had no job, no husband, and ten children. The landlady still had to deal with Sylvia and her kids for another two months, even though I felt in many ways that she had been wronged. The presence of Sylvia's family also meant that the worried landlady couldn't rent out the premises to another tenant and would lose income she desperately needed. It would cost her a lot to paint the apartment, and I didn't get the feeling she had been blatantly negligent in not fixing it up. Unlike many cases I handled, this wasn't a clear-cut case of inequity. The landlady did not fit the stereotype of an absentee landlord taking advantage of a tenant.

I haven't forgotten this case. I also have not forgotten the clerk who referred to me as a secretary. He never forgot me either. From then on, whenever I came to that particular courtroom he made a point of greeting me with, "Good morning, counselor."

Virginia Martinez graduated from the De Paul University Law School in Chicago. In addition to her legal aid work, she also has practiced as a civil rights lawyer, and in a general practice. Martinez is currently executive director of Mujeres Latinas en Acción, which provides social services to Hispanic women in Chicago.

2

The Right Reason for Going to Law School

Randa Zagzoug

Around the time I received the letter informing me that I had been accepted as an asylum officer for the U.S. Immigration Service, I thought I'd never hear the end of it.

"Is this why you went to law school?" asked my friends and colleagues, many of whom were just starting their legal careers in tax and bankruptcy practices. They turned up their noses, their eyes squinting at me in disbelief. Looking back, I have to admit they had a point. Spending three months of my first year out of law school in Guantanamo Bay, Cuba, to process Haitian refugees wasn't what I had envisioned doing with a law degree.

Unlike those who went to law school because they liked the courtroom theatrics of litigation or the prospect of making a lot of money, I went for another reason: I was shy. I thought getting a law degree and practicing law would force me to be assertive and teach me to begin speaking up—if not for my rights, at least for other people's. When I arrived at law school in 1987, I had no idea where a law degree would take me.

Soon after beginning law school, I knew that I was offended by most types of law practice. In my view, lawyers seemed to be constantly profiting from other people's misery. The person seeking legal counsel either has been accused of doing something wrong or feels he or she has been wronged by someone else. The only winners in a blame game, in my opinion, are lost tempers and frustration.

Product-liability lawyers, especially, rubbed me wrong. They didn't seem to be suing to force manufacturers to make a safer product as much as to have a shot at a contingency fee. And though I believed criminal defendants were entitled to legal representation, I just could never stomach representing someone I *knew* was a criminal. To me, it was all so distasteful.

At law school I found that one area of the law seemed to me somehow more positive than others: immigration law. It wasn't about closing a deal, sticking it to a *Fortune* 500 corporation, or trying to salvage the life of a mangled accident victim. Immigration law enabled its practitioner actually to change another person's destiny. It was about giving people a second chance, the clichéd "new lease on life."

Having come to the United States from Egypt at the age of seven, I felt my personal history enabled me to bring sensitivity and heartfelt commitment to my work as an immigration lawyer and provide me with an outlet to use my skills for the good of others. If I could help people escape misery and live productive lives in a new country, I would be making a small difference in the world. After more than two years of practice, I persist in my optimism that as an immigration lawyer I can have a positive effect on the lives of genuine refugees.

I soon had the chance to combine my inclinations with my legal training. During the second half of my first year out of law school I was chosen as the lawyer to lead a group of twenty-three asylum officers to Guantanamo Bay, where the U.S. Immigration and Naturalization Service (INS), the federal agency that oversees immigration matters, had set up a camp to process the thousands of refugees who were then fleeing strife-torn Haiti.

As a lawyer, my job was to review and monitor the asylum officers' caseload to ensure that proper legal and procedural standards were being applied to each applicant's case. I was in effect the quality assurance officer and examined literally thousands of applications during those three months. Occasionally, I would ask an officer to qualify his report. The purpose wasn't to take the officer to task but to clarify the justification for a conclusion.

During the screening process, which consisted mainly of a personal interview, asylum officers tried above all to ascertain the credibility of the applicant before ruling on the merits of the case. Key elements of credibility were the consistency of the applicant's story and circumstances faced in the home country. We were looking for consistency in the oral testimony and the plausibility of the account, given conditions prevailing in the country.

During screening, asylum officers also had to be careful not to read too much into certain behavior by the applicants. In many instances, we learned, an applicant's demeanor can be a function of culture rather than a predictable indicator of credibility. For instance, eye contact between speakers generally is considered a sign of trustworthiness in Western culture. We are taught at an early age to look someone in the eyes when he or she speaks to us. In other cultures—and sometimes our own—eye contact may be avoided for many reasons. It may be the product of shame in the facts about to be related. It also may be the product of respect, since in some cultures one may not look directly at an authority figure.

Decisions often are difficult to make. Sometimes the most affable applicants have the most unmeritorious claims. On the other hand, some of the most loathsome, arrogant applicants have the most compelling stories of oppression to recount. Of course, it is most gratifying when I interview an applicant who not only meets the legal standard but whom I sense is also "deserving" of the protection of the law.

Occasionally I was compelled to deny an application to a Haitian who revealed he assisted in the "necklacing" of another person, that is, placing a gas-soaked tire around someone's neck and lighting it. That person probably was disqualified even if he had otherwise convinced the asylum officer he might face persecution if returned to the island. U.S. immigration laws are not intended to protect those who violate other people's rights.

I also had to be clued in to the structure of Haitian society and the subtleties of political and religious organization and overlap. That required specialized knowledge. For example, if an asylum officer knew an applicant's church exposed him or her to political persecution—churches often had cells functioning as opposition to the government—the officer had a duty to note it and use it in determining the applicant's fate. Belonging to a particular church often is a political act in Haiti and could cost refugees their lives if they went back. Such information could strengthen an applicant's case even though the applicant might not be aware of its significance.

During the time I spent in Guantanamo Bay, I conducted some interviews with those seeking asylum to get a feel for the process. I recall the first one I did. It was one that reinforced my faith in the process.

As the applicant entered the yellow canvas tent,

I was surprised at what a good presentation he made. Clad in a patterned sweater, slacks, and black dress shoes, he was miles from the image I had of the tattered clothes and sun-ruined skin of a boat person. It reminded me of the touching daily sight of the clothes the migrants had hung out to dry on the barbed wire that prevented their escape. I wore a purple tie-dyed jumpsuit. The refugees were suspicious of anybody in a uniform, and business clothes might be viewed as a uniform.

The interpreter, who translated the whole thirty-five-minute exchange, sat next to me across the table from the man I was interviewing. I explained through the interpreter that everything he told me would be held in strictest confidence.

"Did you understand the introduction?" I asked the applicant. "If you don't understand, tell me and I'll rephrase it."

At first this applicant's demeanor was unflappable, his face expressionless. He responded with little emotion to the preliminary questions.

"What is your name?"

"Antoine," he answered.

"How old are you?" This could be a difficult question. Many of the refugees didn't know their age. Often, age had to be established by asking how many Easters they had experienced or by figuring it out in relation to a family member or friend in the camp whose age we already knew. Antoine knew his age.

"Nineteen," he said.

"Where did you live?"

"Do you have any family in the camp?"

With the preliminaries out of the way, I began to ask him about the events leading up to his arrival at the camp.

Antoine said he had been a grass-roots poll worker for the former president's party. In detail, he described the polling process and how his house in a pro-democracy stronghold of Port-au-Prince had been used as a polling site. He described the voter registration cards he had handed out and enumerated the planks of platform of the party he supported.

I asked him about his political activities, and he said he "belonged to a group," which meant that he was politically involved. I pressed him for details; he spelled out the party's acronym and then repeated them for emphasis. Not only did he know what the letters stood for but he also was politically savvy enough to know to take down the posters from his house that would mark him as belonging to a certain side.

Throughout the interview, he looked me directly in the eyes. He bobbed his head emphatically and gesticulated as he talked. At one point, he pounded on the table to drive home a point. It was as if he had been waiting his whole life for someone to ask him to tell his story. To me, at least, his behavior seemed driven by sincerity. As with all credible applicants, here was either a true refugee or a spectacular thespian. Since his testimony was detailed and specific and squared with what we knew of his local area in Haiti, I judged him a legitimate candidate for asylum.

I couldn't let Antoine see it, but inside I was elated to be speaking with—and it was hoped helping—someone who I sensed was fleeing persecution. It confirmed my reasons for doing the work I did.

During the three months I was forced to become a shrewd judge of character, I would like to think I became sensitized to separating people who truly needed our help from those who were trying to pull the wool over our eyes.

Today my work continues as an asylum officer and lawyer for the INS. Occasionally I think back to the skepticism of those who wondered about what I was doing with my law degree. I wasn't certain then, but I think about the work I did in Guantanamo Bay and the work I do now, and I say to myself, "This is precisely why I went to law school."

Randa Zagzoug, a graduate of Seton Hall University Law School in Newark, New Jersey, works for the Immigration and Naturalization Service in Newark.

3

The Glamour of Corporate Law—Sleeping on the Floor

Robert Zochowski

Corporate lawyers, especially those in New York City, carry an almost romantic reputation for burning the midnight oil. Movies, television, and other images in our popular culture portray dapper men and women in tortoiseshell spectacles poring intensely over masses of documents, their ties and scarves loosened and take-out food littering the desks and coffee tables.

Occasionally the corporate lawyer's life does approximate the Hollywood stereotype. But as I learned during the first year, nothing in law school, except perhaps the process of cramming for final exams, prepares the novice associate for this experience.

One Monday afternoon late in my first year of practicing law, word came from a client that a transaction that had been on the back burner was ready to close. The buyer and seller would be in the office in two days to hammer it out. As is often the case in transactions lawyers handle, we had prepared papers in a rush for a quick closing, only to have the principals bog down in additional negotiations. Other assignments had occupied my mind, and the same was true for the other lawyers on the transaction team. Now and then we heard rumblings that the deal would soon close, but nothing had materialized for months.

As a result, we didn't take news of an imminent closing all that seriously. We lawyers suspected it would be another week, probably longer, before the two parties were ready to embark on the back-breaking negotiations we knew were in the offing.

Wrong! On Wednesday the parties arrived at our midtown Manhattan offices from the West Coast and informed us that they were prepared to camp out in New York until the deal was completed. Our team, consisting of a lead partner, a senior associate, and myself, was thrust into advising and producing documents to finance the purchase of offshore oil-production platforms. At this point, all the documentation we had consisted of our original drafts of the financing agreement and the mortgages. Given the changes in the structure of the deal over the last half year, we would need to make massive revisions. Moreover, we had to finish the tremendous amount of "due diligence" that must be completed before the transaction could be closed. This included reviewing all the underlying contracts related to the assets being purchased, structuring the partnerships that would legally hold the assets, and preparing governmental filings. Much of this due diligence had been identified early in the transaction and was complete or nearly so, but reviewing the legal problems associated with such work and ironing out miscellaneous problems ordinarily takes weeks to complete.

I had never seen a deal like this, with its unfamiliar oil company assets and innovative financing structure.

I had reviewed drafts of the financing documents but still did not have a good understanding of how everything was supposed to work. While various representatives of the two parties and the bankers thrashed out the deal in conference rooms, I got busy as the person responsible for making the changes in the hundreds of pages of documents. It wasn't glamorous; for two days my job consisted largely of shuttling between conference rooms and my office, inserting and deleting clauses and terms at the direction of the senior attorneys. Because things were moving at such breakneck speed, the senior lawyers had time only to give orders, with no time left to offer anything more than cursory guidance to an overwhelmed junior associate.

The senior associate and partner were immersed in doling out advice to our client, the bank was busy financing the deal, and I seemed to be flying solo, producing and reviewing the documents. Often I made a change in one section of the documents and had to decide what changes were necessary elsewhere.

The pressure was extraordinary. For the first time in my rookie career I was truly responsible for looking after the client's interest, and ultimately the return of the money it was lending. However, I didn't have the time I would have liked to double-check my work. If I missed something, very likely it would not be caught until after the transaction had been agreed to by the parties—or worse.

So this became my schedule: From 9:00 A.M. Wednesday until early Thursday morning I worked nonstop. Pizza and Chinese take-outs were my sustenance and an office floor my bed. At 5:00 A.M. Thursday, after twenty straight hours of concentration, I stretched out on the carpeted office floor near my desk for a few hours of sleep. A seat cushion from the lobby chair served as my pillow and my overcoat as a blanket.

At 8:30 A.M. Thursday, I dived in anew, reviewing and fixing the documents. By 10:00 P.M. Thursday I was exhausted, with no end in sight for the work that needed to be done. I was having tremendous difficulty focusing on what I was doing as I moved into my second consecutive all-nighter. I returned to my office floor at 6:00 A.M. Friday to snatch several hours of sleep.

At 9:00 A.M., I returned to the closing room to continue my work. I was completely exhausted and truly unable to keep my head clear. Suddenly the parties came to an impasse over some remaining issues, and for two hours it appeared the deal might die. At one point, certain deal makers were heard screaming at each other behind closed doors. Secretly I hoped for a delay. It would give me the chance to review what I had done over the past two days and look over some things. I was not so lucky.

The remaining obstacles were cleared by 1:00 P.M. Final terms were agreed to and the parties left our offices. It was time for me to go home for the first time in three days. Though I'd managed a single shower, I was clad in the same clothes I'd worn to work Wednesday.

I was more tired than I had ever been and completely stressed out. Never before had such responsibility been thrown at me. As I drove home, I continually second-guessed myself, questioning how I had resolved issues that had come up and wondering whether I should have taken a second look at a document or tried to focus the partner's attention on something. By the time I reached home, I was numb. I was certain that I had missed things—things that I thought would cost me my job.

Later that same night I received a call to come back to the office Saturday afternoon to clean up the documents and to prepare the sets of documents for execution first thing Monday morning.

I had to go back, retrace my steps, and forget

the nice day off I had been envisioning. Forget the game on TV. Forget my wife and kids. So I traveled to the office, playing my mental tapes yet again, what brainpower I had remaining centered not on the task at hand but how I was going to find a new job. Maybe I should buy the *New York Times* first and look at the want ads. I was convinced that when the partner reviewed the papers he would find glaring errors, though I had no idea what they might be. Growing more and more unnerved, I hesitated as I approached the threshold of the partner's door. I entered his office, trying my best to hide my panic.

The partner greeted me perfunctorily. What was up? Without betraying the anger or stress that I was certain he was feeling, he launched right into the task at hand.

We didn't exchange much in the way of pleasantries, but he didn't throw me out either. He told me he had reviewed the transaction documents I had prepared over the past three days. "Under the circumstances, it wouldn't be unusual to miss things," he said. "But basically, everything looks pretty good." Everything looks pretty good! I couldn't believe it. The guy told me everything looks pretty good. I suddenly felt much more alert and infinitely relieved. Needless to say, I didn't lose my job and, in fact, logged another eighteen hours that weekend assembling all of the papers.

At first, a new lawyer can be awed by the millions of dollars involved in a major corporate transaction. The novice must put out of his mind the prominent names of the companies and financial institutions involved and the huge amounts of money involved, and keep up with the rapid progression of events. A bargain is reached between the principals after hours of tense negotiations during which egos and dollars are on the line. To an observer, the evolution of a high-stakes business transaction and the lawyer's role in it potentially make for riveting drama. But I was in this one for real and didn't have much time to savor its unfolding.

Good as these experiences are for the soul, unfortunately they are all too frequent. The fast pace of the transactions, the heavy workloads of senior associates and partners, and client sensitivity to large legal bills frequently result in new attorneys being pulled into a deal in its very last stages, at a point when there is simply a need for more "bodies" to close the deal. Seldom does a junior attorney see a transaction from the very beginning, which might allow him or her to get to know the principals and grasp all the subtleties of the deal.

Since that transaction, I have pulled many more all-nighters, worked under far more intense pressure, and gained significantly more responsibility. In retrospect, my inexperience during this transaction placed me under more pressure than anything else, because I lacked a feeling for the ebb and flow of the deal and a sense of what issues could be addressed later and what absolutely had to be done prior to closing. Some call this method of training "sink or swim." It isn't easy, and it isn't kind to those who sink, but in many ways there simply is no other way to gain the experience and perspective necessary to mature as a large-firm corporate lawyer.

Robert Zochowski is a graduate of the New York University Law School. A banking-law specialist, Zochowski has practiced law for five years in New York City.

4

Justice for a Guilty Country Boy

Sue Kessler

Brian and I had more than a little in common. For starters, we both were involved in our first felony case. Brian as a defendant and I as a defense attorney—his defense attorney. Second, we both were nervous as hell, Brian because he was facing jail time and a criminal record, and I because I had his future in my hands—and it didn't seem there was much I could do for him.

The teenager was explaining to me in a shaky voice how he came to require my services. As Brian told it, he and an older, conniving coworker had carted off some recycled scrap metal from the warehouse where they worked, sold the scrap, and split the proceeds, each netting about $575. The older employee had enlisted Brian to abet him in the caper and then assuaged his qualms, telling him that the operation was perfectly legal. Geez, I thought to myself as I listened, where is this guy's common sense? The scheme was so transparent they were begging to get caught.

Brian was befuddled and frightened. Recently he had moved from a small town in southwestern Virginia to the "big city" of Richmond to take the warehouse job. To a jaded urbanite, Brian's youth and naïveté would have been refreshing. To a criminal mind, however, Brian was the perfect accomplice: he was a small-town boy and not too smart.

Brian had no previous police record, but the evidence against him and his colleague was overwhelming. The man who had written the check to the two defendants had identified them in a police lineup after finding it unusual when they explained they were doing the company a favor on their own time by getting rid of the metal. Having listened to Brian's story that day in the courtroom, I realized it was unlikely any jury would be convinced by any defense I could concoct. The best service I could do for Brian would be to keep him out of jail rather than try to help him beat the charge. I advised him to plead guilty. He'd have a criminal record, but at least he wouldn't risk years in prison.

"You should have—could have—been smarter than this," I told Brian the first time we met. Maybe I was talking to myself.

I was having a difficult time of it. Six months out of law school I had recently "hung out a shingle" and had a small office that I shared with several other lawyers. I was hurting, almost desperate for clients. Some days I had so little to do, I literally sat around the office waiting and hoping that the phone would ring. I had perceived criminal law as the most glamorous and lucrative area of the law. For an experienced practitioner, perhaps that's true. I was starting out. My bank account and confidence weren't exactly bulging.

The day I was assigned to Brian's case, I had been reconnoitering the courthouse like a scout, hoping a judge would appoint me to represent an indigent defendant, trying to find work as a court-appointed attorney. By taking on court-appointed cases for defendants who couldn't afford a lawyer, I would gain the experience that would enable me to build a practice. I also would surmount that catch-22 that haunts all novices in the job marketplace; everybody said I lacked experience, but no one was willing to give me any.

Asking around to find out about potential cases and land clients, I heard about Brian. Here was a case with two defendants being charged in the same crime. Codefendants often have conflicting stories—and therefore conflicting interests—and need to have separate attorneys. I realized that Brian probably would need a lawyer because there likely would be a conflict between these two defendants. I slipped into the courtroom, sat in the front row during Brian's arraignment, and caught the judge's eye. I was appointed. The other defendant's attorney, I noted, was a Mr. Taylor, a former federal prosecutor, a respected Richmond defense lawyer and familiar face in the city's courtrooms.

At a preliminary hearing, Mr. Taylor appeared to be angling to pin the blame on my client. Instead of concentrating on refuting specific allegations against his client, as it seemed to me was his duty, he repeatedly focused the hearing on Brian's actions. It was my client, he told the judge, who had loaded the scrap into the truck and who had driven it to the scrap dealer. I didn't think much of Mr. Taylor's efforts to malign Brian, but I should have. At the next hearing a month later, Brian pleaded guilty to a charge of grand larceny. Sentencing was set for another month hence.

Brian was assigned a probation officer whose job was to prepare a presentence report, which is presented to a judge to help him impose an appropriate sentence. Among other things, the reports contain a family history, a victim-impact study, a criminal history, and information about the offense. Several days before the sentencing, Brian and I were preparing for his appearance before the judge. I was reviewing the presentence when I discovered the most astounding fact. "Well, look at that," I said to Brian. "We've been had." There in print was the information that Brian's partner in crime somehow had gotten the prosecutor's office to drop the charges against him. The ringleader of this hapless two-person ring had gone free, and my client was about to end up with a criminal record.

I don't think Brian fully grasped the significance of his "partner" getting off the hook. My young client was a sincere kid with an honest soul who just wasn't all that bright. He was ready to go to jail if that was what the judge decided. I, his attorney, understood what I was looking at and appreciated the mess Brian would be in if he pleaded guilty; just because he would not go to prison didn't mean the case wouldn't have repercussions. Brian still would be a convict. As such, he would lose his civil rights; he wouldn't be able to vote or hold a passport.

This was not right. I had to do something—I would not allow my client to take the rap for a crime he had not conceived and could not have carried out by himself. He knew now that what he had done was wrong. He had learned his lesson. Soon to be a convicted felon, Brian was entitled to fair treatment at least by the authorities, if not their compassion.

I didn't know how the other guy in the case had escaped facing the music, nor did I care at that moment. More important than answering the question How had this happened? was answering the question How can I make things right for Brian? Somehow I had to find a way to expose the unfair treatment he had received.

I called the detective on the case. "Did you know the prosecutor's office had decided not to prosecute the codefendant?" I asked him. "I was told I wouldn't be needed as a witness in this case," he said. He assumed Mr. Taylor's client had pleaded guilty or that "something had been worked out." The detective acknowledged that he thought it stank that my client had taken the blame even when he wasn't the primary architect of the crime. "He's at least as guilty, if not more so," he said of Mr. Taylor's client.

A lightbulb went on in my head. I asked the detective to testify to what he had just said to me. My only chance to get Brian cleared would be to show that he had been treated unfairly by the prosecutor. It wasn't much of a defense at this late stage, but it was worth a try.

This was a sensitive situation, however. Defense lawyers don't usually find themselves in the position of calling police officers for help, and cops understandably don't normally enjoy undoing their cases. But the detective understood that Brian had been wronged and agreed to testify for me at the hearing.

At Brian's sentencing hearing, I put the detective on the stand. Reading from the presentence report, I noted that the grand larceny charges had been dropped against the other defendant, taking care to point out that my client had already pleaded guilty to the exact allegations. I asked the detective if he could think of any reason that should be so. No, he said, and repeated his assessment of the other defendant's guilt in conceiving the scheme.

It took only a few moments for the judge to grasp the significance of the detective's testimony, that for whatever reason, my client was not treated fairly by the prosecutor's office. The judge began shaking his head, slowly, from side to side. He looked disgusted.

"I'm dismissing the charges," he said to me. To Brian, he said, "You're free to go."

Brian and his girlfriend erupted into tears, which were followed by hugs and kisses. The two of them danced about the courtroom.

It had been an unorthodox move for me to put a police officer on the stand. I knew his testimony would paint the prosecutor and the codefendant's attorney in a bad light. It would make Mr. Taylor look as if he had cut a back-room deal for his client, which is exactly what I believe happened. As the new kid on the block, I didn't want to earn an early reputation as a troublemaker, but I had to do right by my client.

It was gutsy of the detective to testify for me—normally, it's the cop trying to put the defendant behind bars. That detective did the honorable thing and I was grateful to him.

Asking a police officer to exonerate my client told me I was making progress as a lawyer. I had taken an unusual approach to help my client, and it had paid off. The statute books weren't going to help me on this one. I had reacted to a situation that to me represented an injustice, even if it had been done to someone who had admitted having committed a crime. It was a long shot. Of course, I had no idea that putting the detective on the stand would get Brian off the hook so easily. I had just wanted to get him a fair hearing, to get the "injustice" aired publicly.

I recently represented a client charged with embezzling money from his employer. As with Brian, this client had acted like an idiot and was paying the price. Unlike Brian, there was no evidence that this guy had committed the crime, just that he had acted stupidly enough to make himself a suspect. Remembering Brian's case, a highlight of my first year as a lawyer, helped me guide yet another person through the criminal justice system. The man accused of embezzling might have ended up in jail, but a country boy in Virginia had shown me that there is more than one way to deal with a case.

I never found out exactly why or how the charges were dropped against Brian's codefendant. Later, I surmised that the defense lawyer had a friend in the prosecutor's office who owed him a favor. It didn't really matter. Lesson learned: Even criminals are entitled to fair treatment.

Sue Kessler, a lawyer for fourteen years, is a graduate of Tulane University Law School in New Orleans, Louisiana. Today she works for a law firm in Richmond, Virginia, where she has a criminal and civil litigation practice.

5

A Lesson in Justice

David Dominguez

The words pouring out of Mr. Stephens's mouth weren't adequately conveying the frustration he felt, and his movements seemed to be trying to compensate. Eyelashes fluttered like butterfly wings about his dilated pupils. His legs crossed and uncrossed, as if operated by puppet strings. In between crossings, the feet beneath his chair shuffled back and forth, and his body seemed to contort as he recounted his tales of injustice.

Mr. Stephens was in my office to wage war against his union, and he thought of me, a first-year staff attorney for the National Labor Relations Board (NLRB), as his personal tank, his fighter jet, and his destroyer.

He had filed a charge alleging that the union had wrongly passed him over for a union position with an employer. The job Mr. Stephens thought himself entitled to was a plum—steady work, great pay. Government investigators thought he had a case, and I had two weeks to prepare for a trial.

But Mr. Stephens's dissatisfaction with the

union went way beyond getting passed over. In his half-hour tirade, he told me about the many things he felt were wrong with the way the union was run—things he wanted me to change.

Mr. Stephens proudly provided the union's motive for denying him the position. Recently he had opposed the reelection of union officials, publicly accusing them of financial improprieties and other misconduct.

He frothed with accusations of corruption and "dirty politics." He wanted the federal government to bring those "corrupt gangsters" finally to justice. Mr. Stephens said he lived for the day when, at long last, the union was going to experience what it felt like to be squashed by a much bigger force, the United States of America. He thought the day had arrived.

This was 1980, and Mr. Stephens said he was impressed by the power—and heartlessness—of a government that had forbidden America's Olympic athletes from competing in the Moscow games.

"When the time finally comes to get on the plane, the president says, 'You're going nowhere,'" he said. If a president could do that, surely the government had the power to clean up union practices, he reasoned.

I was dismayed to see that Mr. Stephens held such an inflated view of what the United States government could do for him. As an administrative law attorney, my primary duty was to prove one minor charge of illegal conduct. I had no power to instigate a full-scale investigation of union hiring practices. I represented the government, not him. I couldn't even call him my client. I would have to explain to him that the complaint the government had filed on his behalf would do little more than get him some back pay.

I wondered about this man. What kind of guy would take on a union by himself? I had doubts about whether his frenetic personality would impress the court. Finally, who would the union's lawyer be? Finding out was just a matter of pawing through the endless government forms. My heart sank with the discovery: Here I was, with the ink on my law school diploma still not quite dry, and I was being opposed by one of the most feared labor attorneys in San Francisco.

This case, in my first year, was weaving me into a bundle of nerves. Yet hadn't I chosen governmental work over other alternatives? Eager to join forces with the "feds," I was game to throw myself into the firing line. I was drawn to this work by the promise that government attorneys are not introduced "slowly but surely" into administrative litigation but rather immersed all at once. Most important, my idealism told me that no law firm had as much power as the United States government to make positive changes.

After reviewing the file, I calmed myself with a silent prayer. I called the employer's attorney. She was reluctant to speak with me and made it clear that her client would do nothing to antagonize the union. I made it equally plain that I was calling on behalf of that same federal agency on which her client had so often depended for injunctions against illegal union picketing. The government, I reminded her, had a long memory.

My veiled threat delivered, I assured her that the government would protect the employer's relationship with the union by forcing the employer to testify only under subpoena. She sensed that I was doing what I could to help the employer save face with the union and threw me a bone. Confidentially and "off the record," she confirmed that Mr. Stephens should have gotten the nod.

I hung up, feeling invigorated by this discovery. I was more convinced than ever that I enjoyed an advantage over my classmates who had joined private firms. After all, I was helping to right wrongs.

Still, I remained cautious about Stephens's case, and I was growing concerned about his temperament. Stephens refused to lower his expectations of my capabilities. In our meetings, he conveyed how he relished the prospect of seeing union officials sweat and squirm on the witness stand during cross-examination. He broke into a broad grin as he imagined the union president, humiliated and overwhelmed by guilt, apologizing to him on the stand for the union's abuse of authority.

My uneasiness returned. Did Mr. Stephens really think that the NLRB could bring the union to its knees because of his narrow charge? I had to rein in his enthusiasm or there could be trouble.

I started slowly, explaining to him that there was no chance that the union president would apologize. If the union lost, I told him candidly, it would claim that there was a misunderstanding but no intentional wrongdoing. Any monetary award would be limited to the difference between what he would have earned in the job he was denied and the amount he earned doing other work in the meantime. And, I told him, if he won, the union would get slapped with an order insisting that it not repeat the violation.

For the first time, Mr. Stephens had nothing immediate to say; he was incredulous. After a moment, his twisted face reflected a question: How could he be so wronged yet be offered only a few dollars and a piece of paper? He had burned so many bridges, alienating the union establishment and many "friends," by filing this charge. Did I expect he'd ever get work again if the government didn't straighten out the entire mess? he asked. I think he may have realized for the first time that he was in too deep.

I felt torn and more than a little guilty. I was tempted to continue delivering all the rehearsed lines about providing legal representation free of charge to the public but that I was limited by what the law permitted us to do. However, I felt something was strangely amiss. Here was a young African-American man in his mid-twenties, who had spent his youth successfully maneuvering the violent streets of Hunter's Point in San Francisco. I, of similar age and of Chicano-Latino descent, likewise emerged from a tough inner-city ghetto in Los Angeles. Inside, my instincts were finding empathy in his frustration. We shared a belief that the mighty United States government could bring justice.

His view, it dawned on me, had been my own before I went to law school, where students are trained to rivet on the most slender, narrow facts—to fill the appropriate cubbyhole. One example of this is the idea of standing. The law doesn't allow just anybody to correct an injustice. Only someone who has been hurt—a person with standing—can bring a case to court. While a single case can have a widespread impact when it gets to the appellate level, the prime objective of most cases is to solve a dispute between two parties.

In silence, I studied Stephens's face. He was shaken, profoundly disappointed. Just recently I was proud to wear the mantle of government trial attorney, enjoying my "advantage" over the employer's attorney. Could I now own up to Mr. Stephens that despite all we had in common, I had assumed a status that not only granted privileges but imposed serious limitations as well? I had to be prepared to admit to Stephens that, as much as we both wanted to believe otherwise, the government can't reform society's shortcomings in a courtroom.

My turmoil grew as I charged ahead with trial preparation, deposing and developing evidence to show that Stephens was intentionally bypassed. I was determined to do all I could to build a fire of protest that would encourage other members to come forward if they had been wronged. Maybe, as I tapped into Mr. Stephens's courage and determination, I would find a way to correct the union's wrongful practice after all.

Several days before trial was scheduled to begin came the breakthrough that I both feared and welcomed. The union attorney proposed that the matter be settled. Mr. Stephens would receive lost wages and benefits and be placed at the top of the out-of-work list. In exchange, the union would not admit any wrongdoing. When Mr. Stephens appeared in my office later that day to discuss the settlement offer, I was excited for him. I figured once the word got around that he had been able to get the union to agree to even more than the government could have secured through formal litigation, it would encourage others to stand up for fair treatment.

Mr. Stephens rejected the offer out-of-hand. He wanted nothing to do with terms that did not include the union's admission that it had violated his federal rights. He felt that going to trial was far better because it would publicly expose the union's betrayal of trust and formally preserve the misconduct in a trial record. His rejection of the settlement meant I would have to argue before the judge.

The trial was a disaster. All of my pretrial questioning of supportive witnesses was undone through the labor attorney's cross-examination. At first Mr. Stephens's unemployed colleagues confirmed many of the details of his account. But then, inexplicably, they began adding new details that hurt Stephens's case. Indignation suddenly gripped me. Outraged, I presented these apparently defecting witnesses with their pretrial affidavits (written sworn statements) and pressed them to explain how this new information was conspicuously absent from them. Delivering a further blow to my case, they testified that government agents had allowed them to say only that which would build the case and that it was the union attorney who finally gave them a chance to tell the whole story.

Why did they embellish their testimony? Had promises been made? Had they been threatened? As the trial attorney, I surely should have been able to summon the government's power to force these witnesses to tell the truth! Then at least we could prevail on the narrow issue before the judge.

However, I lost the case and Mr. Stephens stood alone. As he turned to look at me, I could feel his anger and bitterness. His pained expression brought to mind the agitated state he had been in during our first meeting, when he raved about the injustice of the president keeping the

U.S. Olympians home, denying them their day in the sun. And then it struck me; I had denied Mr. Stephens his chance to shine by not taking seriously his desire to obtain justice for himself and fellow union members. He hadn't asked me for any guarantees. But he had asked me to support his cause. When he asked me to help him rally his union peers around him by informing them of their rights, I had declined, saying I would stick to the narrow issue of his case rather than try to change the union.

I had been wrong to limit my own horizons. From that point on, I was a lot more sensitive both to the larger issues in any case I took and to the individual needs of my clients. I always tried to remain open to the possibility of using the narrow scope of any case to effect broader changes. For the next eight years as a government lawyer I aimed to educate clients and others as well as to litigate grievances. If a client enlisted me to make others aware of issues connected to the case, I obliged. Perhaps the lessons of that case have something to do with my becoming a law professor. Sure, Mr. Stephens was a little crazy, but he ensured that I always remember my sense of justice.

David Dominguez graduated from the University of California at Berkeley Law School fourteen years ago and teaches law at Brigham Young University Law School in Utah.

6

The Imperfection of Law and the Death of Lilly

Ji-Zhou Zhou

"Autopsy?" inquired the dead woman's father, in Chinese. Peering at me, he seemed uncertain about whether to render his thought as a full-blown question. "Should we conduct an autopsy on my daughter?" I discerned a sense of guilt and hesitation in the way he pronounced the word *autopsy* in reference to Lilly.

Next to me, silently suffering, sat the husband the dead woman, Lilly, had left behind. He was a skinny man, and he trembled throughout the meeting, which had been called to discuss how to address the messy legal legacy of her death. With me was my more experienced co-counsel, Greg, a respected personal injury lawyer. Although I was there in my capacity as a lawyer, nonlegal thoughts kept intruding while I concentrated on doing my job. My mind strayed to the broken-hearted husband and the young daughter he would have to raise alone.

"Autopsy?" the father asked again.

I turned to Greg and translated the question into English. "Do you think we should have an autopsy done?"

Greg leaned back in his armchair and emitted a deep sigh. "You are asking a very personal question." He paused. "It is so personal that I cannot even answer it. But if it were my wife, I wouldn't do it, for sure. No."

"From the perspective of an attorney, will you suggest one way or the other?" the father prodded Greg, probably fearing a yes. I made the translation, and this time Greg spoke as a lawyer.

"What an autopsy does, usually, is to identify the cause of death. In this case, the cause is clear. An autopsy may or may not discover evidence of medical malpractice. But if we find out for sure there was no malpractice, your case is over. Plus, do you know what they do to the body? They don't even try to put it back together again after the autopsy is complete."

I didn't translate the portion of the conversation about cutting up the body into pieces. It would be too painful for the family. Though neither the woman's father nor husband spoke English, I sensed they intuitively understood the painful delicacy of the conversation taking place. The issue of an autopsy was dropped. A period of silence ensued while Lilly's grieving husband buried his face in his hands. Her father stared at the floor, motionless. I felt hearts were bleeding.

Just days earlier, Lilly had been killed riding her bicycle to the university, where she taught and studied. Witnesses said the accident appeared to be the driver's fault, not Lilly's. She was an outstanding student who had struggled against the odds in her Communist homeland and to get an advanced degree in the United States. Lilly recently had been offered a job as a professor in Hong Kong, and the family was to leave in two weeks.

"Forty thousand dollars in annual income. Forty thousand dollars. That was what she was going to be paid," her father would tell me later. He had continued, "She said to me, 'Dad, we don't need to settle for the cheapest of things anymore. We don't need to check around to see which grocery store offers the cheapest food. With my income we can go to a restaurant once in a while, too.' " His voice and face dropped. I saw his lips trembling. He could hardly pronounce the last few words.

After the accident, we discovered that the driver of the van was a part-time hairdresser, earning minimum wage and having few assets. The driver did maintain a minimum $15,000 insurance policy as required by law. The bereaved family refused to accept that amount to settle the case: They wanted to file a complaint and get a judgment against the van driver, even though I had made them aware of the possibility that she would certainly file for bankruptcy and thus be spared having to pay any damages. America's legal system and business interests toyed with the family's fate. The Chinese consulate was reluctant to help, arguing that Lilly was a Chinese student privately sponsored in the United States at the time of her death, even though she was an employee for the Foreign Affairs Department before coming to pursue her doctorate.

I had been referred to Lilly's family by a relative, who told me that the family feared the hospital where Lilly's saga had abruptly ended would try to garnish its bank account for the $40,000 in medical bills. This family needed legal help and they needed it quickly.

As the family's lawyer and language conduit, my job was to inform them of their legal rights and advise them on a strategy for recovering any money they were entitled to for their daughter's unexpected death. I felt a singular sense of responsibility and commitment in this case. Not only was this family having to contend with the loss of a loved one in foreign surroundings but also Lilly had been the primary breadwinner. The family was faced with paying the medical bills as well as trying to figure out a way to get money to live on in the future.

When I first spoke with them, they clearly were barely able to deal with their loss let alone confront the daunting possibility of a protracted legal case. Though most nonlawyers know little of the nuances of what the law entitles them to, they have at least a vague sense of what a lawyer can do for them. It was my job to determine strategy: to find out whether there was a claim warranted in this situation. I had to figure out if we should file against the van driver for negligence, the ambulance driver, or even the attending physicians.

At the meeting, I asked Lilly's father if he would consider petitioning for political asylum in the United States based on his fear of persecution for providing service to the American army during World War II and having contacted old friends after coming to the United States. He said he would think about it, but he hadn't given me an answer. I think, somehow, it wasn't easy for him to cut off all ties to the place where he was born, grew up, and suffered—at least not without a sense of loss for the land he certainly still loved.

As a lawyer in this case, I not only had the duty of explaining to the family its legal options but I also functioned as a cultural bridge between Greg and the family, on the one hand, and the family and the U.S. legal system on the other.

For instance, I was called upon to tell the family why the county attorney's office, after investigating the accident, declined to bring murder charges against the van driver. It was necessary to have a basic discussion of the concept and meaning of murder. I explained that Western legal traditions, and specifically in the United States, generally require intent or extraordinary disregard for another's life for an act of killing to be considered a murder.

After the conference, I drove the father and husband home, and they insisted on my going into their apartment to have a cup of tea.

A cute little girl of about six opened the door for us. As soon as Lilly's father sat down, she jumped into his lap.

"Grandpa, what did the lawyer say about my mommy? Can Mommy come back to dance with me? Why can't she come back?" she asked, either not clearly understanding that her mother had died or perhaps not yet comprehending the finality of death. The grandfather stroked her shining jet black hair gently, incapable of speaking. He had seemed to handle things better in the office. Once home, it was as if something in him collapsed.

"You are back! Oh! You are back." A voice came from the hallway leading to the bedrooms. Then I saw a gray-haired old lady, her failing vision fixed on me.

Lilly's mother began speaking to me, and it soon became clear that she was confusing me with someone else—Lilly's best friend, as it turned out. "How do you know so quickly? You must have taken a plane here. But I still don't understand how that could happen to her." She grabbed my hands and started to weep.

Her husband answered. "No. This lady is not our daughter's friend. She is the lawyer." He gave me an apologetic smile. "She is the lawyer," he emphasized, "who is helping us in the case."

He turned to me. "Lilly's mother has suffered from heart disease for years, and last year we found out her brain shrank a quarter. With my daughter gone so suddenly, I am afraid she may not survive either."

I didn't know whether Lilly's mother was following the conversation, and I felt uncomfortable talking about her problems in her presence. She moved slowly to the couch and settled herself there.

The little girl hopped off her grandfather's lap and bounded up onto her grandmother's. "Grandma, don't cry. Please don't cry." She wiped off her grandmother's tears. "Mommy must be hiding underneath the bed," she said. Tears dropped from the little girl's beautiful brown eyes.

I picked her up and held her tightly in my arms, fighting back a choking in my throat, and brushed away my own tears.

Then the husband emerged from his bedroom with Lilly's diploma and a couple of picture albums that contained photos they both took in different countries when she worked as a United Nations interpreter before studying in the United States. I took the red-covered diploma from the table. The diploma was identical to the one I received more than ten years ago in China when I had graduated from the university, just after the upheaval of China's cultural revolution. Holding the diploma in hand, I suddenly realized the long way she had come in pursuing advanced studies. I understood every single thing in life she had to sacrifice for her career, every single step at the expense of life's enjoyments. All of a sudden she seemed so familiar that I felt as though I knew Lilly. I knew this woman.

My desire to remain professional and detached finally failed me, and I stood still in the center of the living room and let the tears roll down my face in streams.

Later, as I prepared to depart, Lilly's father accompanied me to the door.

"We were just a very regular family in China. We didn't have other opportunities except for this daughter. She is the reason we are all here today. Whatever compensation the law allows is not going to compensate me for losing my dear daughter." His face was shining with grief. "My little granddaughter will certainly grow up, even without her mother. My son-in-law can remarry. We will get old and die," he said quietly, sadly. And then, more rhetorically: "But what is to vindicate my daughter's death?"

I fled to my car and sat in its comforting darkness. My hands were shaking so much that at first I couldn't find the ignition hole. Three years of law school equipped me with legal principles, logic, and analytical skills. But no amount of law school and training, with or without the rigorous Socratic method, could have prepared me for this.

The supremacy of law seemed to lose its omnipotence and seemed somehow deficient and perhaps a little useless. There was so little solace the law could provide to a family that had lost its only hope in life—a daughter who would have provided a lifetime support for her parents, a wife who would have filled the void in the life of her husband, and a mother whose love for her little girl could never be replaced.

My thoughts brought to mind a discussion I had eight years ago with one of my best friends, a respected Chinese lawyer, before coming to the United States. He said that sometimes he felt helpless witnessing his clients' dilemmas, and all he could do was to be sensitive and sympathetic as a friend, even though that accomplished little.

On this occasion, I looked out the windshield and saw the father still standing under the citrus tree where I had left him. His white hair was fluffy in the evening breeze of late November. The street lights shone down on his shoulders, forming a shadow—a prolonged silhouette of infirmity on the parking lot. Then I abruptly drove away and turned down a quiet street, where I parked and pondered about Lilly for a long time.

Ji-Zhou Zhou, born in China, is a graduate of Brigham Young University's School of Law in Provo, Utah. She is a writer and legal consultant for the city of Phoenix, Arizona, on international projects.

7

A Case of Life and Death

Suzanne Boxer

As I entered the courtroom, a woman leaned toward me and, smiling, extended a leaflet. I was somewhat surprised—after all, this wasn't an airport—but accepted it and began skimming the front cover. I suddenly remembered the case before the court that day and shoved it under the papers on my clipboard.

The woman's smile was welcoming and also meaningful. She belonged to a religious order that forbade medical intervention and served as a reminder that today's hearing wouldn't involve the usual divorce or child support proceeding I had grown used to during my four months working as a clerk in Family Court. In the most memorable and certainly most poignant case of my first year out of law school, a mother and father were to ask a judge to deny their child the medical treatment she needed to have any hope of surviving a terminal illness.

The parents recently had discovered that their child was sick and were asking the court to let them take her home to face God's judgment—life or death—with the minimal medical intervention their religious teachings allowed. Meanwhile, the hospital's doctors had taken the position that the child, their patient, should remain in the medical center because the parents wouldn't provide the care she needed. Room for compromise in this case was sparse, almost nonexistent; the stakes were as high as they could be. Caught in the middle of the parents, the doctors, and the law were Judge Johnson and me—and our conflicted emotions. Tears, rage, distrust, and even the occasional terroristic threat have come to be commonplace in Family Court. During my first months on the job, I had developed a somewhat thick skin to avoid personal involvement in the high emotions that often course through courtrooms. In this case, I wasn't able to do that.

I took my seat at the base of the judge's elevated platform and took stock of the parties. I noticed that the parents' attorney, a woman, was clad in a conservative floral print dress with a frilled collar and appeared to be about eight months pregnant. Beside her, the parents sat proud but demure, occasionally whispering to their attorney while the hospital's attorney and doctors studied their notes. It was easy to discern which side had a personal stake in the outcome of the case. Behind me, I felt the serious presence of the normally lighthearted Judge Johnson. I also felt an unaccustomed gravity attaching to my role in the case. I would, after all, be doing the legal research for the case and preparing a draft opinion for the judge.

The hearing, which took an entire day, went off without incident. The rationalistic demands of the legal process mostly tried to mask the sentiments present in the courtroom. Whenever Judge Johnson called a recess, you could almost hear a collective sigh of relief, so heavily did the proceedings weigh on those present.

During one recess, the couple's lawyer approached me and introduced herself along with the mother and father of the child. The mother produced a game smile, but I could tell she was suffering. The father, wearing a dark suit, was kind and very polite, but his mind, too, was elsewhere.

At first, I was hesitant to speak with the parents and their lawyer, feeling it might be inappropriate to have any contact lest I develop an emotional attachment or some kind of sympathy for them and their case. Since nobody raised the case, we chatted like people thrown together in a room, idling away the time. After that initial meeting, we spoke no more.

Later the father took the stand, pleading his case before the judge. Under questioning from the parents' attorney, he explained the religious basis for his and his wife's position. He spoke with restrained passion, if such speech is possible. He appeared comfortable in the courtroom setting, as if he had been exposed to things legal. As for the mother, she had carried the child and seemed to be bearing the burden of the child's impending death as well.

The judge had briefed me on the case before we entered court and I remember feeling sad for this couple before walking into the courtroom, never knowing how much sadder I would feel later. They were two people who felt they were doing their best for their child, but who were facing the burden of denying their child the medical care she needed.

Later, as the doctors described to the court the painful and intrusive treatment that was planned for the toddler, I wondered whether it was always worth trying to save a life at any cost. How, I thought to myself, could doctors know better than parents, and how could the judge know better than everyone? The treatment for the child would be awful for her and for her siblings, who would have to watch the devastating side effects of the torturous treatments.

After the hearing, my confusion was in full bloom. The parents appeared to be loving, nurturing people. Both were articulate and well educated—a far cry from my preconceived notions of religious zealots awaiting the apparition of a deity to save their child.

The case clearly was affecting the usually jovial Judge Johnson. In this case, the judge was transformed into a full-fledged legal scholar with rumpled hair and furrowed brow. I was surprised and confused by his change in demeanor. The jokes ended, as did our accustomed discussions of that week's movie highlights. This case made everyone associated with it stop and think.

Often, Judge Johnson had a good idea how he was going to rule based on pretrial pleadings and clued me in on the general direction he wanted my legal brief to take before any testimony had been heard. It was intimidating at first to have a judge tell you that a certain case should have a certain outcome and that as a clerk you must find the law that will allow for the judge's decision. Sometimes I was confused when there was strong case law on either side. I had to develop the fine art of underplaying the merits of the outcome the judge didn't want. While law school tends to teach one how to argue any side of a case, it hadn't prepared me to confront the gray area of personal morality at the core of this child's case. In this case, I couldn't get a sense of what the judge thought was the appropriate outcome.

The pregnancy of the parents' lawyer added another angle to the drama in the courtroom, I thought. Here was a soon-to-be mother arguing another woman's right essentially to allow her child to die. Later, as I struggled internally with what I felt should have been done, I wondered how the lawyer would feel if she had been a disinterested member of the public rather than a legal advocate. Would her own religious beliefs allow her to decide such a fate for her own child?

Would she, as I sensed many people would do, shake her head in disbelief at the parents' position if she read about the case in the newspaper?

All these conflicting feelings swirled about inside me as I sat down to write a draft for the judge the next day. There was no time to waste, because a life was hanging in the balance. I knew what the case law said, but the testimony I heard a day earlier made me wish I could reinterpret case law in a whole new way that would satisfy both sides.

So little had passed between us, the family and myself, but as I was the person who would write the draft opinion in this case, I felt the awful onus of power that I bore in this case. Here I was, just out of law school and contributing in a very tangible way to a case of life or death. Perhaps in an effort to relieve my burden, I decided to write a draft with every imaginable argument. But the parents had a legal problem, as I was to discover when I began researching the case. Just a month earlier, they had rushed their child to the hospital for emergency treatment. Legally, their position was inconsistent, and the judge had no choice but to rule against them. Usually it's anathema to a judge to be overruled by an appellate court, but I sensed that this was one case in which Judge Johnson wouldn't mind seeing his ruling overturned.

A month later, the judge called me into his office to tell me that the little girl had died. I never saw or met the child. All I knew about her was what I had learned in the hearing. She had brothers and sisters and parents who clearly cared about her welfare but who felt the fate of the child was in God's hands. She had been the object of everyone's prayers and best wishes in addition to the medical community's best efforts. It was not enough. I don't know what the court system could have done for the child. All I know was that I felt bad.

After hearing of the child's death, I felt like I should do something, anything, to let the parents know I was sorry. Perhaps I should send them an anonymous note of condolence, perhaps some flowers. It felt strange to be so intimately involved with the family's life, to have helped make a decision on what to do with their child, and yet stand aloof when they experienced their final sorrow. Yet I knew there was nothing I could do. I had had a hand in the legal process and it would be totally inappropriate for me to express any feelings one way or the other. Feeling depressed and empty, I walked up the stairs to my private little corner office where I could be alone. I shut the door and cried for several minutes.

I never read the pamphlet I was given before the hearing, but I still remember being torn between my duties as a representative of the court and a person who could sympathize with the parents' wishes. Today, I still think about that case, and the memory of the family lingers with me as no case has then or since. I remember my brief personal contact with the family, the way they treated me like a human being, so unlike the rationalistic way the court had treated the family and the fate of its child.

This case made me realize that our system of jurisprudence isn't perfect. I realized that a court and a judge—indeed the whole legal apparatus—can be dedicated to dispensing justice but restricted by the straitjacket of statute and precedent.

Suzanne Boxer, a graduate of the Emory University School of Law in Atlanta, has a special interest in family law and represents custodial parents as an assistant district attorney in Philadelphia.

8

The Judge Who Taught Me to Teach

Laurie Levenson

Judge Hunter didn't just hire his law clerks; he adopted them. During my first year out of law school, I was lucky to be one of his "children." As a newly graduated law student, I had moved three thousand miles from my home in sunny Southern California and needed all the family I could find.

Even as I acclimated to the gritty streets of Camden, New Jersey, I had some idea that I wanted to teach law. In college I had started out as a premed student. After struggling through chemistry but discovering I enjoyed political science, I took some more prelaw courses. Concepts of justice won out over test tubes: I decided to enroll in law school. There I found my hungry mind challenged by the abstract nature of legal theories. Later, during my first year as a law clerk, I found I loved researching cases and solving legal puzzles. Until I met Judge Hunter, the law for me was not much more than an intellectual game. With his guidance, I discovered that it is so much more. Judge Hunter held definite opinions about the road I should take to become a law professor, and we would have many discussions about how I should get there. However, my first day on the job was full of more mundane concerns than what I was going to do with the rest of my professional life.

Entering the federal courthouse that first day, my nose was assaulted by a smell redolent of rotting tomatoes. It turned out that the odor came from the Campbell soup factory that until recently dominated the Camden skyline. All courthouse employees became rapidly inured to the "flavor of the day" that wafted into our nostrils from the plant two blocks away.

I worked with two other clerks, both of whose personalities were as shocking to my system as was the revved-up East Coast lifestyle. There was the New Yorker who spoke so fast I caught only every third word he uttered, and the Chicagoan, a large friendly fellow who, like a bodyguard, escorted my five-foot-tall frame around Camden's intimidating streets. As clerks, our task was to read briefs written by the lawyers and prepare memoranda with a recommended ruling for the judge. Our memos included a concise synopsis of the facts of the case and an explanation of the state of the law on the issues in dispute.

When I walked into the judge's chambers that

first day, the two clerks were hunched over several piles of court files. My new colleagues already had divided between themselves the very sexy criminal and corporate cases. I was like a vulture, arriving just in time for the scraps.

"This one looks right for you," said one, and a file was handed to me. It was a case involving an international tax dispute. I knew very little about U.S. tax law at the time, let alone anything about how a foreign company might fare in the eyes of Uncle Sam. But I soon warmed to the case. If the lawyers can write it, I thought, I can figure out what they're saying. An obscure point of tax law was the kind of legal challenge I thrived on.

Later, when oral arguments in the tax case were held before Judge Hunter's panel of judges, I noticed that one of the lawyers in the case made his presentation in a near-catatonic state. With a blank face and a pitchless voice he droned on, appearing to go through the motions of arguing his client's case but not really having his heart in it. I'll never know if that lawyer's disengaged state stemmed from nervousness or lack of interest in what he was doing. But his demeanor made an impression on me during that first year as I began noticing other lawyers often seemed unenthusiastic about the cases they presented. The lawyers' attitudes got me thinking about what I wanted to accomplish as a teacher and early on gave me a sense of mission. One thing I realized then, almost a decade before I was to become a full-time professor, was that I would strive not just to impart to my future students textbook matter but also to instill in them, if I could, a love for law as I loved and appreciated it.

During the course of the year, I grew stronger in my conviction that I wanted to teach. The question I frequently discussed with Judge Hunter was whether I should go straight into teaching at the end of my clerkship. Judge Hunter said the best law professors have "real-world" experience and suggested I learn about the problems real people face in the courtroom by becoming a trial lawyer. He encouraged me to see for myself the effect of laws on people's lives. If I went straight into teaching, law would remain a board game, a college library research project. By actually practicing law, I could shape and polish a tool for making people's lives better. Working as a practicing lawyer, I realized, obviously would also result in a better learning experience for my students. I was gradually getting the message: Without real-world experience, I'd end up something like the disaffected, unmotivated lawyers who were, in my mind, examples of what not to be.

"Whatever you want to do, work with the people and see what the practice of law is really like," advised Judge Hunter. "You know, Laurie, if you still want to be a teacher after you've done that, you'll still be able to teach. And you'll be a much better teacher," I remember him saying. The realization crystallized with gentle prodding from the judge.

Judge Hunter's approach wasn't always so philosophical, however. He was a stickler for moving cases along at a rapid clip. And did we move cases! It took some appellate judges, with their fine-printed footnotes and stabs at judicial immortality, as long as two years to dispose of cases, but Judge Hunter's cases received rulings in as few as two months and rarely longer than four.

The goal of our office was not to publish the smartest or most grandiosely worded opinion. It was to arrive at thoroughly researched decisions as fast as possible so that the people who were affected by our rulings could get on with their lives. Judge Hunter's point was that the legal system existed principally for the parties using it—the public—and only secondarily for judges and lawyers using it as a forum to set legal precedents and make statements about the ideal nature of the social contract.

"Our responsibility is to decide the case in the way that we think is right—right because we believe it to be right—and not because the Supreme Court might disagree," the judge wrote in a memorable dissent.

Judge Hunter's background as a U.S. Marine meant he sometimes spoke in code. To his clerks the word *garrot* meant keep it close to the vest. It was his way of telling us to keep mum on discussions involving cases.

The judge rarely took himself too seriously. When his clerks ate meals at his house, he would proudly point at a picture of himself and a former Miss New Jersey that was displayed in the family kitchen. Judge Hunter also had the most amazing way of resolving a prickly situation without putting anyone in an awkward position. When we clerks told him that another judge's clerks were being worked to death and needed a break, Judge Hunter called the slavedriver and invited him to a leisurely lunch, thereby giving the clerks an afternoon breather.

Out in the real world, I soon reaped the fruits of Judge Hunter's wise advice. It was while I moonlighted as an adjunct law professor that I began applying the lessons I learned from the judge. While a prosecutor, I got a jury to convict a man whom inmates in a prison had nicknamed Punchy. The sobriquet was somewhat of an understatement, given that Punchy had a penchant for killing people. While in jail, Punchy fashioned weapons from whatever he could get his hands on. From sharp typewriter cartridge spokes he made the stiletto he used to kill someone who brought him his food in solitary confinement. He also soldered together metal plates from a desk and made an ax that I received as a memento of my days at the U.S. attorney's office. Today, that ax is one of my most effective teaching tools. Every now and then in an evidence lecture, my students' attention will flag. I'll brandish the ax and tell the story of Punchy. Seeing a real weapon and hearing the story of a person who sits behind bars as I speak in class heightens interest by bringing the courtroom into the classroom. My students are able to see that the law is alive.

Judge Hunter is no longer alive, but his lessons affect the way I teach and the way I think about my work. I learned both from the way he did things and the things he said. His suggestion that I get real-world experience has made me a better teacher. By working as a prosecutor, I collected real-life experiences, such as the story of Punchy, to share with my students. Judge Hunter's feeling that the law didn't have to be a grind but could be used to genuinely better people's lives also stayed with me. And the judge's military background instilled in me the idea of honor and duty: a responsibility to my students and my profession.

Judge Hunter was more than a boss and a friend. He was my teacher.

Laurie Levenson graduated from the UCLA Law School in Los Angeles. She teaches criminal law, evidence, and ethics at Loyola University Law School in Los Angeles. Levenson appeared on Cable News Network as an analyst during the Rodney King police brutality cases.

9

Lambing and Lawyering

Merle Raph

"Your witness," the opposing lawyer said. I rose to my feet, pursed my lips, and squinted at the lines on the yellow legal pad I held. I looked at the other attorney. Finally I looked at the witness.

Cross-examination. I dreaded the prospect of cross-examining this witness, an expert for the opposition. She probably had more in-court experience as a witness than I had as a lawyer. Several months out of law school, I was making one of my first court appearances. As I approached the bench, I was unnerved to notice that she was studying *me.* She had my number.

The witness smiled as I prepared to ask the first question. I cleared my throat and told her who I was and who I represented. She seemed relaxed and amused at the discomfort I evidently was intimating.

I presented my first question to her and she fended it off without any difficulty. I wasn't prepared for her deft response. I heard my voice rising and shaking a little as I fired off several more questions at her. Her poise was remarkable. Her head rose and fell, as if she were suppressing a yawn. She disagreed with everything, and I could establish nothing from her testimony. This was probably the worst job of questioning a witness Judge McPhillips had ever seen in his thirty years on the bench, I thought, with much embarrassment. I was embarrassed all right. I'd clerked for the judge for three years. In his rural Montana courtroom, a fumbling attorney had a high profile. There was no crowd into which I could melt.

Everyone in the courtroom seemed to know I was foundering. The defense attorney lolled at his table. He probably couldn't believe his luck. The empty gallery was witnessing either the thwarting of a young buck freshman lawyer by a great witness or the helpless flailings of a newborn, very green attorney. Whichever it was, the court reporter was enjoying it. He had the anticipatory grin of a vulture watching slow death in the desert. The reporter leaned back in his chair, threw a look at the witness, and placed his pen in his teeth as if it were a congratulatory cigar.

I grew hotter by the minute as I stood there. I glanced back at my client and saw the concern blanketing her face. She leaned forward in her chair, resting her hands on the table, her fingers interlaced. Disgusted. I was in double trouble. I was a panicked rookie, *and* my client had lost faith in me. It had been a risk for her to hire me. She thought I would get her grievance a fair hearing, and here I was getting her case barbecued.

Judge McPhillips came to my rescue. He leaned forward in his chair and said in a monotone, "Counselor, do you have any more questions?"

"Yes, Your Honor," I stammered. Blank. My mind went blank. Where is the door? was the only thought my mind could muster. Remembering what I now know to be the time-tested advice of my trial professor, I spoke up.

"Your Honor, it's awfully close to lunch, could we have a recess?" I managed.

"Well, counselor, there's ten minutes left till lunch," he began, and, as I was about to sink to my knees and beg for the blessed recess, "but I guess we'll break for lunch and we'll continue at one-fifteen."

I was in shock and I needed air. My client just turned and walked out of the courtroom without saying a word. Gathering up my papers, I left the courthouse and drove out to my ranch to regroup. Well, not exactly "my" ranch, and it was no Texas spread, but still a much loved refuge.

A high school friend, Michael, and I together own a small farm of 120 sheep and four cows. Arriving there, I walked through the small herd of sheep. It was early spring and the middle of lambing season. It was my turn to check for any ewes having difficulty giving birth.

Lambs, like human beings, normally are born headfirst. Their heads emerge with their front legs tucked under their chins. Once in a while something goes wrong and the lamb gets stuck with only one leg out or winds up in a breech position with the lamb completely backward in the birth canal. The ewe labors and tries to force the birth, and death can result for both the ewe and the lamb without human assistance. Making my rounds I spotted one ewe near the fence. She was down on the ground and breathing heavily, a clue that she was having a difficult labor. I watched her for about five minutes. She lay on the ground next to a clearing she had made in preparation for her offspring. Nothing was happening. Walking back to my car to put coveralls over my suit, I tried to forget about the trial but the image of standing there frozen in the courtroom would not disappear. "Dumb, dumb, stupid!" I mumbled under my breath, aspirating the last word with a vengeance as I pulled on the coveralls.

As I approached the ewe, I knelt down, rolled up my sleeve, and zipped up the coveralls, unaware that my tie was hanging out front. I had lubricated my arm by lathering it in soap. I pushed the lamb's head back into its mother, grabbed hold of its front legs, and pulled out the lamb. Minutes later, I repeated the procedure to produce a second lamb. The ewe recovered quickly and began to clean her lambs as I stood there to observe. At least something went right today, I thought as I wiped my arm clean with a towel. My partner Mike drove up and we exchanged greetings. He agreed to put the ewe and her two new charges in the barn for me because it was ten minutes after one. I had five minutes to get back to the courtroom. I stripped off the coveralls and spent some quality time cleaning my shoes, dreading the return to town and court.

My legal career had begun some six months earlier after I passed the bar exam. I was sworn in before the Montana Supreme Court, and returned to practice in my hometown of Shelby, a small town of three thousand people about thirty miles from the Canadian border, and twenty-five miles away from the nearest town. Within the county's two thousand square miles eight lawyers practice. Wheat, cattle, and oil drive the local economy.

It had not been easy to make the decision to return home after law school. Not only is the pay lower in rural Shelby than in Montana's "urban" areas but small-town attorneys often are held in low esteem by lawyers in such large towns as Helena, the state capital, and Great Falls, neither of which hardly could be considered a teeming metropolis!

As a deputy county prosecutor, I could also have private civil practice on the side. After all, there are only about thirty felony cases a year in the whole county. I had a lot of time to develop my own clientele. Even today much of what I do consists of what I call "dog-and-cat" law. As county prosecutor, I get calls from residents asking why their trash hasn't been picked up or asking me to arrest a neighbor for failing to muzzle a barking dog.

Urban attorneys in large firms have the opportunity to specialize in one area of the law, whereas the rural attorney must be a blue-collar, jack-of-all-trades lawyer.

"Mr. Raph, you may continue," Judge McPhillips said as court resumed. I rose and approached the witness chair, which contained the same witness as before the recess. Needing to establish my own credibility quickly with this witness or face a mutinous client, I employed some advice from a law school trial instructor: Get in the witness's "comfort zone," his term for personal space. Boldly, recklessly perhaps, I strode right up to the railing in front of the witness and leaned forward. I fired off a question. The witness, who had played me like a fiddle just an hour earlier, looked horrified. She leaned way back in the chair as far as she could.

She agreed with the premise of my first question. Emboldened, I articulated another and elicited the response I had sought. The recess spent at the farm had relaxed me, and my self-confidence was returning.

Another inquiry and again a bull's-eye for my client, who must have now been a little relieved to see her attorney earning his keep. Hey, this is great, I'm doing great, I thought to myself as the examination gained speed. The witness mumbled something and looked ill. She's caught, you've got her cornered, I gloated inside. The defense attorney objected to one of my questions.

"Overruled," affirmed the judge, and my hardball attack continued apace. Nothing could stop me. I asked the last couple of questions and the witness agreed with my logic, my conclusions, and my client's positions. Cross-examination? No problem. What a miracle! What a transformation I had undergone since the morning! I strutted back to my table and flipped a nonchalant "Your witness" to my opponent.

Before the defense attorney could speak up, Judge McPhillips requested both attorneys to approach the bench.

As I neared the bench, I could detect a smile under his mustache and a gleam in his eye. He appeared on the verge of bursting with laughter. The defense attorney was from the state's second largest city, Great Falls, and he approached the bench slowly, unsure of what was going on.

Leaning out over the edge of the bench, the judge motioned us to move closer with his index finger. I took two steps forward. "Counselor," the judge said matter-of-factly, "you have afterbirth on your tie. I take it you pulled some lambs at lunch." His face relaxed and he chuckled.

The defense attorney stared at the judge, who was pointing at my tie with his gavel. The attorney's eyes followed the direction of the gavel to my tie and the clear, crusty mucouslike substance that was stuck near its middle. His eyes narrowed and his mouth puckered as if he'd mistakenly swallowed a spoonful of soggy, lukewarm cat food.

Keeping my back to the courtroom, I peeled the dried little globule from my tie with a handkerchief and dropped it inconspicuously into my side jacket pocket. I turned around to walk back to my client. The other attorney watched me walk away but did not move for several moments. "Are you okay?" the judge asked.

"Yeah, yeah," stammered the defense attorney, turning around to go back to his seat.

The trial continued with nothing remarkable taking place. My cross-examination was more than adequate, and I improved with each subsequent witness. The case was settled before the judge could issue a decision.

I've always wondered why the judge didn't halt the proceeding sooner. Judge McPhillips, who has his own ranch with about sixty cows west of town, must have noticed what was on my tie some time before he actually stopped the testimony. When I was his clerk, he used to say to me, "I've seen most everything in court, but I doubt I'll ever see it all." Perhaps this was something he hadn't seen in a courtroom, and he was enjoying it.

Looking back, I can't help laughing at myself. Here I thought I was the fastest-maturing lawyer in Montana history when it turned out I only had one of the state's most soiled ties. It was probably the first and last time a lawyer benefited from not cleaning up after himself! I've always wondered whether my sudden prowess with the witness stemmed solely from a witness rattled by a sullied tie. There's no way I'll ever know for sure.

Yet, lucky as I was that day, there had been something rejuvenating about returning to a farm during the recess. The farm has always been a place of solace for me. Sheep and cows generally do not lie or evade the truth as do self-serving witnesses. The calves and lambs arrive in the world either dead or alive; it doesn't take two days of testimony and hours of conference-room haggling to determine that fact. At the very least, clearing my head would have helped improve my technique. I also learned never to quit. I could have declined to continue cross-examining the witness, conceded, and then just sat down in safety, but instead I relied on some more sage advice from a professor who said that when the witness kicks you right in the stomach, show no emotion, regroup, and go right back at him.

It has been about seven years since that day. In addition to learning the invigorating effect of regrouping, I continue to rely on the other lesson I learned out at the farm. That would be to tuck in your tie before you pull up the zipper on your coveralls.

Merle Raph is a graduate of the University of Montana Law School in Missoula. He has been practicing law for nine years in Shelby, where he is the Toole County attorney.

10

The Inmate of Letters

Susan Emlet Crandall

Roger, convicted as the getaway car driver in an armed robbery, was the most talented felon I ever met. Without a doubt he is the client I remember best during my first year out of law school. I was a legal aid lawyer handling appeals for indigent inmates trying to overturn their convictions. Most of my clients were poor and uneducated. Roger was poor and overeducated.

His handwriting was beautiful. The elegantly curlicued letters transformed the yellow legal sheets he wrote on into florid nineteenth-century manuscripts. Roger had a lot of time to perfect his art. In the late 1960s, prisoners didn't have telephone privileges. He was serving a ten-to-thirty-year sentence at a prison in upstate New York when our correspondence began.

Jan. —, 1969

Mr. Roger L'Ambert, #4890765
———— Correctional Facility
————, New York

Dear Mr. L'Ambert,

I have been assigned as your attorney to pursue an appeal to the Supreme Court, Appellate Division, Second Department, New York. Notice of appeal has been duly filed on your behalf, and your case should be received before the April term of the court.

I will send you a copy of the brief prepared on your behalf. The written record of your guilty plea of November —, 1968, will be provided to our office free of charge following the grant of our motion for procedure *in forma pauperis.*

Please feel free to contact me if you have any questions.

Very truly yours,
Susan Emlet Crandall,
Attorney at law
Legal Aid Society of
Nassau County

January —, 1969

Dear Mrs./Miss Crandall,

I have no confidence in Legal Aid. I know you're just practicing on us so you can become real lawyers. I've never had a lady lawyer before. Are you married?

Let me tell you about myself. I am black, not Negro, and I was born in Suriname in South America. I speak four languages—English, Spanish, French, and Haitian—and I'm working on my second B.A. degree. If I ever get out of here I'm never coming back.

I work out every day. I'm six-foot-two, weigh

175, and guys in here know not to mess with me. I'm pretty impressive (ha, ha). Let me know when you plan to visit, so we can discuss my appeal.

Sincerely,
Roger L'Ambert

February —, 1969

Dear Mr. L'Ambert,

Thank you for your letter and the background information you provided. I expect that your appeal will involve only the issue of excessive sentence, as your conviction was based on a plea of guilty. The information regarding your many accomplishments will not be relevant in the appeal, unfortunately, as we may raise only issues that appear on the record. That is, the factors determining your sentence were presented to the trial judge and cannot be raised again on appeal.

I expect to begin research on your case in the near future and will be in contact with you by mail. I regret that it is not possible to visit our clients personally.

Very truly yours,
Susan Emlet Crandall,
Attorney at law
Legal Aid Society of
Nassau County

February —, 1969

Dear Ms. Crandall,

You don't have to tell me it's a worthless appeal. I'm working on another angle. There's a guy who used to play professional basketball for the ——

who knows about my case. He wrote to me the last time I was in and now he's trying to get me a scholarship to the State University of New York out on Long Island. Here's his name and number: A., 444-4444.

You've probably found out that I have three prior felonies, but they were all for check-kiting. This one is a bum rap. I was outside in the car while three guys went into a bar—they were supposed to be buying some beer, but next thing I knew they held up the place. I got caught in the car with a gun and stuck with robbery; ten to thirty years. You know, we were about 100 yards the other side of the Queens border—over there I would have gotten about two to five.

Anyway, I'd like to get out of here and start school this summer. See what you can do for me with my friend.

Hopefully,
Roger

March —, 1969

Dear Mr. L'Ambert,

I have enclosed letters of recommendation prepared by A. and myself, which have been forwarded along with your records to the State University of New York. Once your acceptance is verified, a special application will be made to the parole board at ——, which will involve a personal appearance by you.

As you suggested, I have researched the issue of appearance by counsel at parole hearings, and there is no precedent for such a right as a matter of law. However, I have prepared the enclosed brief arguing for such a right. Please let me know your comments.

Very truly yours,
(Mrs.) Susan Emlet Crandall,
Attorney at law
Legal Aid Society of
Nassau County

April —, 1969

Dear Mrs. Crandall,
So sorry to hear that you're married. A. told me he met you. He plans to sponsor me before the parole board, so the fact that they denied my demand for counsel won't be so important. I'm pretty optimistic. Once I'm out of here, I'm straight forever.

Thanks anyway for the brief. Maybe you can appeal that issue some other time.

Ever faithfully,
Roger

A. successfully pleaded for Roger's release at the parole hearing. Soon after the following letter, Roger began calling me at the office. Stuart, my husband, and I befriended him. The letters, however, continued.

June —, 1969

Dear Susan (Can I call you that?),
So when are you coming to say hello? I've been elected president of the dorm council and they're having a Bar-B-Que next Saturday—why don't

you and Stuart come out? (Do you socialize with ex-clients? Ha, ha.) Call me and let me know if you can make it.

Love,
Roger

June —, 1969

Roger L'Ambert
SUNY at ——, Chelsea Dorm

Dear Roger,

Thanks so much for the tour of campus, dinner, and party—we had a great time. I was impressed with the impact you have on people you've met in such a short time at school. Your charisma is amazing.

When you come to town next month, give us a call—we'd like to return the hospitality.

Sincerely,
Susan

July —, 1969

Dear Susan and Stuart,

What a great dinner! I didn't know lawyers could cook. It's been a long time since I ate so well.

I really enjoyed talking to you guys. I realize it sounds like a strange ambition—to want to be the Numbers King in Brooklyn—but you have to understand where I started out. Money still looks good to me, and security, too.

Speaking of which, I've got my dream car: a candy-apple red 1966 Caddy—you won't believe it. I'll drive by 68th Street one day and show you.

Thanks again for dinner. You're fine folks.

Your friend,
Roger

August —, 1969

Dear Susan and Stuart,

Listen, I really need some quick help. I called you all weekend, but you weren't home, so I'm sending this. The dorm faculty adviser has been on my tail about my car—I forgot to mention that my parole officer doesn't allow me to own a car, so it's in a friend's name.

This guy—the dorm adviser—is also bugging me about selling cocaine. Believe me, that is not my thing. Call me as soon as you can.

Hastily,
Roger

August —, 1969

Mrs. Susan Crandall, Attorney at Law
Legal Aid Society of New York, Nassau County

Dear Mrs. Crandall,

I am informed that you have represented Mr. Roger L'Ambert in a matter relating to his parole.

Please be informed that Mr. L'Ambert is in custody in ——, Long Island, charged with felonious assault against a police officer: he was arrested 8/—/69 on the SUNY campus after a confrontation with an officer in which he wrestled the officer's gun away and threatened him with it.

Enclosed is a letter from Mr. L'Ambert.

A. C. Walton
Department of Corrections
———, Long Island

Dear Susan,

I really blew it this time. It's strange how it happened. I just got started with the cocaine thing because of the money, and it got away from me. What an easy way to make it big—even easier than the numbers.

The cop was a jerk—I couldn't help taking his gun away just to show him. I guess you guys were out of town last week. Remember when we talked about what jail was like? You and Stuart said I almost seemed to miss it. I wonder if I did.

Soulfully,

Roger

Roger was a joy to spend time with. His reservoir of knowledge enlightened, and his charisma charmed my husband and me just as surely as it charmed everybody he came in contact with. He was, however, one of a series of unpredictable clients whose actions instilled in me a healthy skepticism.

I don't know what it was with Roger. I guess he just didn't see any options in the real world. He was one of the few people who had the brains and the drive to make it outside jail. He had contacts. Yet he conspired to throw marbles under his feet.

During my second year as a lawyer, Roger, apparently relieved to be back in prison, and I continued to write to each other. He liked the routine of prison life, although he complained that the prison library wasn't up to his standards. What he couldn't do in society without messing up, he managed under the watchful eyes of the guards. He wrote that he was enrolled in correspondence schools for German and electronics. All the more mail for him, I thought to myself. I know he enjoyed writing letters and I'm sure, like all of us, he liked receiving them.

Susan Emlet Crandall, a lawyer for twenty-six years, graduated from the Fordham University School of Law in New York City. Today she works as a public-interest lawyer in San Jose, California, where she specializes in impact cases; those likely to have an effect on a great number of people.

11

The Cop, the "Perp," and the Rookie Prosecutor

Neil Kornfeld

Officer Barber, no stranger to a courtroom, grinned at me. "Counselor, don't worry. Everything will work out," he said confidently.

The cop was a veteran officer who'd been giving me nothing but a hard time since I'd been assigned this minor drug possession case a few weeks earlier. This was my first jury trial, and Officer Barber would be the first witness I'd ever put on the witness stand.

Barber and I walked to the courtroom together. We discussed the case for several minutes more in the dimly lit hallway, when a court officer told us to hustle inside. The judge was waiting.

"Just tell the truth," I advised him as we entered the courtroom. I could ask no more of him, and no less.

As a rookie assistant district attorney in Manhattan, I had been exposed early to Officer Barber's cavalier manner. I wasn't too sure I could rely on him. On this day, he'd arrived more than two hours late. Not one to panic, I wasn't unnerved by his tardiness. But I was hoping for more cooperation when he testified on the witness stand.

Relations between prosecutors and police are often strained, and such a lack of endearment wasn't unusual, especially when an officer was dealing with a rookie prosecutor. He must have felt a little like a guinea pig.

As in most criminal court cases, this one had a police officer as its crucial witness. If the jury believed Officer Barber, the defendant probably would be convicted. As the prosecutor, it was my responsibility to prepare the officer to testify at trial. Witnesses have to know what kind of questions to expect on cross-examination and to be prepared for the inevitable objections that interrupt the testimony.

With numerous court appearances under his belt, Officer Barber didn't seem too eager to receive advice from a novice prosecutor.

In our one previous meeting several weeks earlier, Officer Barber hadn't been particularly cooperative, and he had failed to show up for earlier appointments. We had met in the grungy office I shared with three other rookie prosecutors.

Officer Barber walked in and seated himself in front of me. He did not look like the average cop. He was wearing "civvies" and was dressed more like a defendant than a police officer.

The office looked like any typical government office with its metal desks and bursting upholstery. Windows were filmed with grime and looked as if they hadn't been washed in decades. The institutional off-white walls were pockmarked with nail holes once covered by diplomas and framed prints.

A steady traffic of prosecutors, witnesses, and police officers shuttled in and out of the vibrating room. It was never quiet, and at times you could hardly hear yourself speak.

In the midst of the bustle buzzed the usual office laments and curses. Where's the key witness? Why can't the cop properly complete his paperwork? Why did I get stuck with night duty the night of the Christmas party?

With the case file spread out in front of me, I asked Officer Barber to tell me his story.

"The perp had the stuff between his legs and dropped it to the ground when he saw me," he said and stopped talking. I waited for him to elaborate, but details weren't forthcoming. For my purposes, his explanation wasn't enough. I needed to elicit more details so I could present a more persuasive case to the jury.

I had to know where the alleged perpetrator did what he did, how he did it, and whether anybody could substantiate that he did do it.

"Well, where were you?" I asked.

Officer Barber, apparently sensing that I

thought his story was made up, responded sarcastically.

"On the street and I was able to see the defendant."

I knew this wasn't going to be easy, but the officer was proving much tougher than I'd expected. I had to have the whole story. I pressed on and proceeded to bombard Barber with questions about the arrest.

"Approximately how many feet away were you from the defendant? What was the space between you and the defendant? Did you have a clear line of vision? Was the defendant seated or standing? What direction was he facing? How long did you observe him before he dropped the vials to the ground? Were there other people in the area when you made the arrest? Did you speak with anyone at the scene?"

The serious tenor of my questioning, I think, made the officer figure out that I needed his help. The case was only a misdemeanor, a crime such as jumping subway turnstiles or driving drunk. Most misdemeanors are plea-bargained before trial. Officer Barber thought that I was wasting his time.

Barber's behavior reminded me of my first week on the job, when I spent a night on patrol with two police officers. The goal of the ride-along program, which is required of all rookies, is to help the beginning prosecutor understand firsthand the dangers and difficulties of being a cop.

Officers Leonard and Franco were two street-wise New Yorkers. They had been partners for five years and were "tight." Initially they gave me a chilly reception and were reluctant to answer my questions with more than grunts and monosyllables. They didn't want to share the experience of being a police officer with me. Perhaps they thought that I would be unable to empathize with the dangers they faced.

All this was new to me, and I was eager to learn as much as I could that night. I asked them how long they'd been partners, what kind of assignments they usually had, and how long they had been cops. They answered my questions but curtly.

That night we were patrolling a beat in the Washington Heights section of Manhattan, a high-crime area. I didn't have long to wait to experience the pace and precariousness of police life.

I was in the car for all of fifteen seconds when a ten-thirteen code was called over the police radio. It was an officer's call for assistance and a top priority. At first I thought they were putting on a show. I clutched the door and went for a ride. Sixty miles an hour on Manhattan's traffic-clogged grid is a lot faster in a vehicle than it appears to a bystander.

We pulled up in front of a homeless shelter. The officers leaped from the patrol car, guns drawn. Because it was a call for police assistance, there were already six cop cars when we arrived.

There were about a dozen when we left. Cops protect their own. In this case our help wasn't needed. A fellow officer already had broken up a fight.

Later, the officers invited me to accompany them up the stairs to the roof where a shooting had been reported. I followed them up the stairway to the roof door. The officers searched the roof but found no one.

In the final hours of our patrol, a car hit us. The other driver was apologetic—and sober. No damage was done. The cops laughed and sent him on his way.

After a night on the beat with Leonard and Franco, I was genuinely impressed with their professionalism and courage. I appreciated how different a cop's life is from that of most New Yorkers, who go about their lives in relative safety while officers routinely risk theirs. Prosecutors constantly evaluate the legality of police conduct without understanding the reality of being a police officer in an urban environment.

Riding with the officers helped me to realize that it's vital for cops and prosecutors to understand each other for the system to work.

The police make the arrest, speak with witnesses, and investigate the crime. Without a police officer's investigation and testimony, a prosecutor frequently has no case to prosecute. Without a prosecutor, a cop has no one to ensure that his police work can come to fruition in the form of a conviction. Together the two are necessary for a successful prosecution.

Fortunately, cops and prosecutors usually find a way to work together. Accommodations on both sides are necessary. As with any professional relationship, there's always the personal side, and one way the prosecutor can ensure him- or herself a punctual and helpful police witness is to accommodate an officer's schedule.

Cops have odd work hours, but they also have families and schedules like anybody else, and they don't like to be called to testify in court with only a day's notice. Would the officer who just got off a night shift be happy to show up for a court hearing scheduled for 9:00 A.M.?

It's a two-way street. Police help prosecutors by doing good police work. If a police officer fails to read a suspect his or her rights, the case is jeopardized no matter how strong the physical evidence.

Often it's the little things that really matter. A prosecutor is eternally grateful to the police officer who takes the time to write up legible and intellegible reports. For the prosecutor, witnesses' phone numbers are a vital but often forgotten detail. Details can make or sink a case.

On the day of the trial I arrived at my office for an 8:00 A.M. interview with Officer Barber. This time of day my office is quiet and I needed this opportunity to finish preparing my case.

I did not want Officer Barber on the witness stand after speaking with him only once.

Officer Barber didn't show up for two hours. I called up to the courtroom to tell the judge's clerk that I would be late.

As it turned out, we were several hours late. The judge, however, greeted me very politely. I think he knew how upset I was with my witness, so yelling at me wouldn't have accomplished anything.

Officer Barber made the proceeding seem like the most important event in his career. The jury appeared fascinated by this experienced officer and the patient, relaxed way he recounted the incident. The defense attorney, a court-appointed attorney, finished her cross-examination of Officer Barber with the following line of questioning.

"You spoke with the assistant district attorney about this case, didn't you?" Officer Barber responded that he did. The defense attorney went further.

"In fact, the assistant district attorney asked the same questions in his office that he asked you today in court. Isn't that right?"

"Not exactly," Barber responded.

"Well, the assistant district attorney told you how to answer his questions, isn't that right?" Officer Barber, on stage and performing well, looked at the defense attorney as if her question were insulting and un-American. "No, he told me to tell the truth."

Officer Barber had come through for me.

Neil Kornfeld is a graduate of the Boston University School of Law. He worked as an assistant district attorney in New York City for five years. He now works for a law firm in New York City.

12

When Honey Is Better Than Vinegar

Marlon A. Primes

An elderly man, the day's witness, sat quietly. He was watching the arrival of two lawyers: Mr. Jones and me.

As Mr. Jones, his attorney, and I, the opposing counsel, entered the conference room, the man looked up apprehensively. He was polite and friendly but clearly nervous about the impending deposition. I smiled and greeted him perfunctorily but didn't go out of my way to make him feel comfortable. I myself was nervous and preoccupied with how I would perform in this, my first experience in questioning a witness in a formal proceeding.

Like any other neophyte, I had grossly overprepared, spending weeks reading and rereading the voluminous medical records, accident reports, and applicable codes from *Rules of Civil Procedures.*

I was determined to conduct a thorough deposition and not permit Mr. Jones, who had been practicing for decades, to run over me. Even though partners at the large general-practice firm where I worked told me they were too busy to provide me any guidance, I had participated in moot court in law school and watched instructional videos on how to question a witness. I was going to be tough. I was about to learn, however, that toughness in a legal arena, as in life, must be tempered with humanity.

The witness was sworn in, the court reporter nodded her readiness, and I began barking out a battery of questions.

I started by questioning the witness about what he did for a living, his medical history, and his family life—all background questions that lawyers get out of the way early when examining a witness. The man's answers were responsive, and he had no difficulty understanding my queries. His attitude was helpful and the answers frequently were more expansive than I wanted or needed. However, I preferred a talkative witness to a taciturn one.

Once I had gotten the simple stuff, I eased into questions surrounding the car accident that had fated the lawyers, witness, and court reporter to be there that day. The inquisition now centered not on the witness's personhood but on his actions and perceptions and weather conditions the day of the accident.

"Where were you going?" I asked.

"I was making a delivery," he answered, explaining that he was assigned the task while he was in the middle of performing his regular duties at his job. Further exchanges established that the roads were slick and the visibility bad that day.

"Did your employer require you to get the delivery done within a specified period of time?" I probed.

"Yes."

"So you were in a rush, right?" I asked rhetorically, and, inwardly, triumphantly. I was confident that I was on my way to establishing that the accident resulted from the defendant's negligence and not my client's failure to post warning signs at the construction zone where the accident occurred. Yes, things were going well and I was smug about my ability to elicit information from this witness.

I noticed that across the table, the courtly Mr. Jones, who I guessed was about sixty, looked suddenly troubled. Till now, he had said little and objected not at all to my questions. Now he was fidgety and alert. I felt a twinge of foreboding as his face took on the mien of a boxing champion barely hanging on to the ropes after a barrage of surprise punches.

Before I could score a knockout by eliciting damaging information that would highlight the plaintiff's own negligence, Mr. Jones abruptly, and most rudely, I thought, disrupted what had been an orderly proceeding in a voice brimming with apparent annoyance and indignation.

"There is no way my client can remember that

fact," he said, as if he had just that second succeeded in insinuating his own mind into the witness's consciousness.

I was flustered and sternly told Mr. Jones he should not interrupt. "Let the plaintiff answer the question himself," I demanded. "If he does not know, then he alone can say so."

I resumed my questioning. Almost immediately, Mr. Jones, seeing that I was already testy, provoked another argument, this time about the length of the deposition.

"Come on, get along," he said. He seemed to be belittling the significance of my time of questioning in the same way one might dismiss a waif from an imperious presence.

I exploded. I informed Mr. Jones that I was seeking to ascertain relevant issues and that sanctions could be sought for inappropriate conduct at depositions. As if he didn't know.

"We're conducting this deposition pursuant to Federal Rule Twenty-six," I said angrily. No judge would allow a lawyer—not even Mr. Jones—to act in such a way in a courtroom, and I was not about to brook such behavior in one of my cases. Furthermore, the deposition hadn't taken more than an hour, well within reasonable time limits.

I continued contentiously. "I'll take as long as I need," I yelled at him. I had lost my composure.

My threats seemed to temper Mr. Jones's nasty mood, but it became apparent that his outburst had had an effect on the witness, who now was distinctly uncooperative. For the remainder of my questioning, the witness's memory was mush. At times he glared at me if he didn't like a question and his answers became monosyllabic and curt. The witness now observed the cardinal rule that a hostile witness respond literally to a question and give no more or less than is asked for.

About a week later, Mr. Jones and I met again at a deposition at which he would examine one of my witnesses in the same accident case. Amazingly, Mr. Jones's personality had undergone a metamorphosis for this proceeding. Before the deposition, Mr. Jones politely told the witness, my client, "I am only trying to get at the truth. I hope I don't have to keep you here for very long."

My opposing counsel was no longer the boorish ogre who had attempted to ruin my deposition. He was now playing the part of the amiable gentleman, who was simply trying to ensure that justice was rendered fairly. I thought I was going to be sick watching Mr. Jones flash that wry smile, with all the sincerity of a fox entrusted with guarding a henhouse.

My opponent's strategy worked like magic. My client showered Mr. Jones with generously detailed responses, even though I had instructed him on the cardinal rule. The newly sincere and placid Mr. Jones got much more information than he would have had he resorted to being boorish. In fact, I realized that the minimal civility I had shown his client in the first deposition was no match for the measured dose of compassion and zealous humanity he now visited upon my client.

It hit me: At the first deposition, Mr. Jones had triggered a screaming match in order to drive a wedge between his client and myself.

Later, Mr. Jones really showed his experience when settlement negotiations got under way.

While we were talking on the phone, Mr. Jones said, "Marlon, my friend, I am only trying to be reasonable. I think this offer is fair for all sides." He then sighed and said, "Let me tell you a story. You never can tell what juries will do with the facts. I had a case where I thought my client was not liable. You know what the jury awarded? Twenty thousand dollars. Therefore, we should settle this matter and take away the guesswork," he said. "It will help both of us," he insisted gently. Boy, was he a pro. I felt like he was suckering me, but he was so nice about the whole thing!

We eventually did settle the case. After reflecting on my experience with Mr. Jones, I realized that important lessons could be learned from our various encounters. For instance, while Mr. Jones's attempts to disrupt the deposition were to me reprehensible and probably unethical, I had no excuse for losing my cool. I resolved to keep my composure under difficult circumstances, no matter what the opposing lawyer might say. Furthermore, Mr. Jones, in his kindly handling of an opposing witness, demonstrated to me that being friendly and tender with witnesses can pay dividends. One need not always be confrontational with a witness from the other side. Lastly, Mr. Jones's amicable approach to settlement negotiations helped me focus on how and whether I could best help my client by settling the case. Although I didn't believe for a second that Mr. Jones was being altruistic, his calm approach made me more willing to resolve the dispute.

An author in the *Daily Legal News* and *Cleveland Recorder* recently asserted that the practice of law is one-third legal knowledge, one-third common sense, and one-third negotiating and social skills. I agree wholeheartedly with this statement: How unfortunate it was that I had to learn its accuracy on the job. I have no doubt that had Mr. Jones and I not gotten into a screaming match in the first deposition, I would have been able to retain the cooperation of his client. However, a lawyer also must know when to bear down—or perhaps even lightly bully—a witness in order to elicit helpful testimony. The trick is getting to know what tactics are needed to win over different people. Hence the importance of social skills.

As a result of the entire ordeal with Mr. Jones, I learned the hard way that one often is more successful using honey than vinegar. In fact, recently during a tense moment at a settlement conference, I took a page from Mr. Jones's book. I patted a young attorney on the back and said, "Let me tell you a story, my friend."

And the rest is history. Thanks for the lesson, Mr. Jones.

Marlon A. Primes has practiced law for five years since graduating from Georgetown University Law School. He is an assistant U.S. attorney in Cleveland, Ohio, and occasionally speaks to young people about the importance of getting an education.

13

Seaman Bartley Gets the Boot

Robert Visnick

My eyes perused the litany of charges levied against Seaman Bartley. This one caught my attention:

Charge: Violation of the UCMJ, Article 92.

Specification: In that Seaman Bartley was disrespectful in words or deportment to Ensign Wilson, a superior commissioned officer then known to Seaman Bartley to be a superior commissioned officer, to wit; by saying to him, "Stop looking at me. Who do you think you are, Clint Eastwood?"

I hadn't met Seaman Bartley, but I was a big fan of the actor whose name he was said to have spoken. I wasn't sure whether the alleged impertinence was a point in the seaman's favor or a strike against him.

Unfortunately for Seaman Bartley, comparing a superior to Clint Eastwood was the least of the young seaman's supposed transgressions. He wasn't much older than twenty and barely out of boot camp. Judging from the thick case file I was reviewing in the aircraft carrier's cramped legal office, he was a badly behaved young seaman.

I was a first-year judge advocate with the rank of lieutenant—a lawyer in uniform—aboard an aircraft carrier moored in Acapulco's sun-splashed Mexican harbor. I was part of a legal team assigned to handle legal matters involving the aircraft carrier's five-thousand-member crew. The ship's commanding officer was asking me to get Seaman Bartley discharged from the navy.

In the space of a few months, Seaman Bartley had allegedly smoked marijuana and had been UA—short for "unauthorized absence"—the navy's equivalent of AWOL. Worse, he'd recently been accused of punching *another* superior officer in the face. In all, ship officials had lodged some twenty formal complaints against him. In the close quarters that sailors share in their months aboard ship, Seaman Bartley was more than a pest and a churl. He was bad for morale and seemed likely to incite any irritated crew member to violence.

Practicing law off exotic foreign coasts was exciting and smacked of adventure, and was the very reason I had joined the military's lawyer corps. Getting to the aircraft carrier had been a journey worthy of those breathless TV ads for the armed forces. The previous day, I had left the Southern California naval base where I was stationed with about forty other military types aboard a C-9 cargo plane, the military equivalent of a DC-9 commercial aircraft. Like a movie theater, the aircraft's windows were featuring a screening of Mexico's rugged Baja coast.

Andy—my friend and a defense lawyer—and I noticed we were the only passengers wearing military uniforms. No one said anything about it to us, and we didn't think much more about our clothing until we landed.

Upon arrival, however, a Mexican soldier advised us through a translator that we were to change into civilian clothes before leaving the immediate area of the plane. We scooted back aboard and obliged. That was one of my first practical—and potentially lifesaving—lessons as a United States naval lawyer; wear only civilian clothes when off base in a foreign country. Military personnel decked out in their military garb make juicy, conspicuous targets for terrorists.

From the airport we were bused over a series of ridges that encircle Acapulco to the city's harbor. About half a mile out, undulating lazily on ocean swells, was our aircraft carrier. Its 1,000-foot-long bulk dominated a harbor that was also host to some pretty hefty cruise ships. We were ferried to the carrier in the colorful but fading painted wooden boats normally used to transport tourists to their cruise ships.

Once aboard ship, Andy and I began studying cases involving the ship's crew. We would try the cases several weeks later back in California.

Among them was Seaman Bartley's case. To me, his case captured many of the differences that distinguish military law from civilian law.

One of the first things one learns as a military lawyer is that there are procedural and philosophical differences between the civilian and military legal systems. For instance, a ship's commanding officer has almost unlimited power to bring charges against those he commands. Only for murders and other serious crimes is the military equivalent of a grand jury convened to consider charges. If such charges are brought, they are usually tried in a general court-martial. Less serious crimes, those brought by a commanding officer on the advice of his legal counsel, are heard in a *summary,* or special court-martial, the term for a military trial.

While the military system is more authoritarian in nature than the civilian equivalent, military law provides more safeguards for the "accused," as the defendant is known, than do civilian courts. Military law also provides more opportunities for clemency and leniency. The military provides exposure to a wide variety of cases. A judge advocate's duties range from the mundane to representing navy doctors against malpractice claims.

As a military lawyer, I also advised sailors on more personal things—like preparing wills—that reflected the reality of military life. In most cases, the young sailors were not much beyond their teens and had little in the way of possessions or knowledge about their rights. To some of them, it may have seemed unseemly to contemplate death at such an early age. When drafting wills, we military lawyers were careful to include a clause letting the world know this was a member of the U.S. armed forces so that possible survivors would know to check what kind of benefits a sailor's family might be entitled to if the worst happened.

Back in California several weeks later, I was prepared to present Seaman Bartley's prodigious record before a judge. Given the sailor's lengthy rap sheet, I didn't think this case would present much difficulty for me. But within me there lurked as always an uneasiness with my role as a prosecutor. I was more comfortable defending sailors than throwing the book at them. I felt sorry for most of these kids, who usually weren't hardened criminals, and Seaman Bartley was no exception. He evidently was a young person with few personal resources, and I didn't relish my role as someone who was about to deny him what might be his only ticket out of obscurity.

At the same time, I was obligated to carry out the will of the aircraft carrier's captain. Generally, each aircraft carrier's skipper is assigned two legal advisers to counsel him on how to handle infractions of military law. The advisers serve as liaisons between the captain and us, the people who actually try the cases. If the captain wanted me to seek a bad-conduct discharge for Seaman Bartley, it was my job to do my best to see to it that he "got the boot."

Seaman Bartley's case, specifically the Clint Eastwood charge, introduced me to an aspect of military law that I hadn't thought of before. It dawned on me that I was essentially prosecuting Seaman Bartley for something he had said; such an utterance by a civilian might be viewed as spunky or protected under the First Amendment as the right to speak one's mind. However, in the military, where obedience is paramount, it was treated as a criminal matter.

Earlier, Seaman Bartley had agreed to plead guilty at his trial. In exchange, he would not receive a sentence of more than three months in the brig, or military jail. At Seaman Bartley's trial, the military judge would rule on my request for a bad-conduct discharge. Bad conduct wasn't as ignominious as a dishonorable discharge, but it wasn't something you'd want to put high on your résumé. All those present in the courtroom were aware that we likely were witnessing Seaman Bartley's last moments of active duty.

The case got started before the judge. It was Seaman Bartley, Lieutenant Mercer, his defense lawyer, and myself before the judge in the small, on-base military courtroom.

There would be no witnesses, but that didn't mean we'd be out in a jiffy. For, unlike civilian judges, who must rule only on the fairness of a plea bargain, a military judge must undertake a thorough interrogation of the accused to satisfy himself that the accused committed the crime or crimes that led to the pretrial agreement. The judge's close questioning of the accused, known as a providency inquiry, is one of the extra procedural safeguards in military law and is designed to protect the accused and preclude any notions that an accused has been coerced into a confession.

That a lone judge was hearing Seaman Bartley's case was significant. Civilian defendants usually request jury trials when charged with crimes, while the accused is usually content to let a military judge decide his or her fate. Whereas a civil jury might contain an air-conditioner repairman, a physicist, and an accountant, military juries usually consist of officers, who often don't show much sympathy for the accused.

The providency inquiry places an extra burden on the defense lawyer, who must make sure the client understands that the judge is ascertaining guilt and is not befriending the accused. More than one accused sailor has recanted his confession after mistaking a judge's careful questions for an indication that the judge was his ally.

Unfortunately for everyone involved in Seaman Bartley's case, the defense lawyer and her client both were having difficulty coping with the situation. The defense lawyer was even less experienced than I and apparently had spent insufficient time preparing Bartley for his examination before the judge. I could see my opponent was in an awkward position as she did her best to help Seaman Bartley. I also could see that Bartley, who seemed singularly immature and unwilling to make any concessions to social convention, had no idea how to behave in a setting that demanded respect. During the providency hearing, the judge asked Seaman Bartley if he knew it was an officer he had punched. The seaman replied no, prompting his defense lawyer to request a recess. At other times, he started making excuses for his behavior or would shake his head no even as his attorney cued him with a nod of her head. Brother! Tragically for him, I thought to myself, he evidently didn't appreciate the gravity of his situation. The punishment he was about to receive would follow him for the rest of his life. Sympathy was one lesson I took away from my years as a military lawyer. Unlike the civilian world, where representing a client often is reduced to a service in exchange for hard cash, the military is more of a collective enterprise. There was more of a feeling that "We're in this together," even if I was prosecuting the guy.

The proceeding was in its third hour and everyone, it seemed, but Seaman Bartley had a Friday evening appointment to get to. We knew, however, that we were stuck until the judge squeezed the last response out of the accused.

Since I couldn't speed up the proceeding, I took it upon myself to liven it up. I thought of Seaman

Bartley's maligning of my favorite actor, and at one point in the hearing I said, deadpan, "I know what you're thinking, Your Honor. Should you give him six months or only five. By his behavior, he asked for this time in the brig, so go ahead, Your Honor, make his day." What I'd said was a variation of a line out of *Dirty Harry,* starring Clint Eastwood. I couldn't resist. As far as I could tell, no one picked up on either allusion, but I was getting myself through the marathon proceeding in my own way.

Soon enough, Bartley was on his way out of the military with a bad-conduct discharge. Or as we say in the navy, he got the "big chicken dinner." The following Monday morning, I was back in court asking a judge to impose yet another bad-conduct discharge on yet another tough-luck sailor.

Robert Visnick, a graduate of Suffolk University Law School in Boston, was a judge advocate in the United States Navy for six of his nine years as a lawyer before entering private practice. Today he works in the San Diego area, handling military referrals, criminal appeals, and professional liability defense and is a lieutenant commander in the U.S. Navy's reserve corps.

14

Out There on My Own

Gregory D. Winfree

I should have known my working relationship with this partner was going to be difficult. Why did he have me, a newly minted lawyer and inexperienced junior associate, conducting a strategy session for a major client?

"Are you ready, pahdnuh?" Ken Parker kidded me in a faux western drawl just before the session. To say I was ready would have been an understatement. I had spent three weeks, day and night, boning up on the facts of the case. I came prepared to discuss litigation strategies and to outline a method of cataloging the various documents to be produced in the case. However, I wasn't prepared for the fact that though *I* was prepared for the meeting, the partner wasn't. As the ensuing discussion made clear, Parker had yet to take even a peek at the court file.

We were at the offices of our client, a prominent Washington real estate developer. Before announcing ourselves to the receptionist, Parker had given me the once-over. Starting at the top of my head, his eyes scanned south to the soles of my shoes. "We look good," his satisfied smile told me. That was lesson number one in this most instructive of partner-associate experiences; looking good often is paramount, regardless of the amount of time a lawyer devotes to a case.

The meeting with the real estate firm's owners began. Parker listened very intently to what I was saying to the clients, who had been sued in a simple breach of contract case for just over a hundred thousand dollars. While I spoke, I could almost observe Parker's lightning-quick mind piecing together a summation of my scholarship. Sure enough, when I had finished, he proceeded to take the facts and theories it had taken me weeks to master, and synthesized them into a pithy conclusion for our client. He knew his stuff, and I guess he figured that meant he didn't have to do his homework.

A polished litigator, Parker also was one of the firm's legends. At a fit six feet three inches, he was dashing as well as tall. His clothes were impeccably tailored. Rumor had it that he was formerly married to a network television anchor and that he was a one-time college tennis ace and finalist for the Rhodes Scholarship. None of these rumors was ever confirmed, but their unconfirmability merely added to his stature.

This case was to end in humiliation for him, the firm, and me nine months later. But how could I have known that at the time?

My legal career at the large Washington firm started off inauspiciously enough. I spent the first several months doing law-review chores I thought I'd left behind in law school. I was assigned to draft a law journal article that could also be used as a sales pitch for potential clients. Recognition of my contribution was relegated to a footnote, almost as an afterthought. The partners even omitted my middle initial.

The law journal article was theory, and now I was in the middle of real-life litigation. As things began to heat up in the Washington breach-of-contract case, Parker got deeply involved in a protracted copyright trial on the West Coast. The time-zone difference and the intensity of daily trial preparation meant he rarely had time to discuss strategy or find the time to coddle our client. Much of what lawyers do is saying everything's okay even when they haven't the foggiest idea how things are going or will turn out.

While Parker litigated out West, I was occupied with responding to interrogatories—written requests for information—and assembling the documents we would need for a trial. But I got almost no help from Parker, who soon became an absentee partner and colleague. I did almost everything myself. It seemed that Parker felt he was entitled to use associates on the dirty work while *he* concentrated on the glamorous or more visible courtroom litigation. I was happy he depended on me and relied on me, but my schedule was overwhelming.

For three months I took and defended depositions. I argued motions. I worked so feverishly that I rarely had a free weekend and missed every three-day holiday from Presidents' Day through Labor Day. I was a lean, mean litigating machine, or so I thought.

I was making many decisions myself with minimal guidance, especially on matters that required immediate attention. This could be dangerous. Meanwhile, our client was beginning to question whether a junior associate just appeared to be in charge, or actually was.

Things became especially difficult when we were hit with motions that required instant responses. On one occasion I had a single day in which to prepare a response to a motion. The research I had turned up was of no help to our side. I called Parker, but he didn't get back to me until late that day and I didn't see him until just before we appeared in court to argue the motion the next morning.

"If the law is not on your side, argue the facts" was an adage I'd often heard in law school. I argued the facts and defeated the motion, or our case might have been sunk. But I got scant help from Parker.

I could have handled the pressure better if he'd said, "This is your case, run with it." But he couldn't say that, because *he* was the tony lawyer who had been hired by our tony clients, not I.

When he and I did work together, our relationship got downright farcical. During a trip overseas, Parker sat in the last row of the first-class cabin and I in the first row of economy seats directly behind him. Parker had the heart to slip me some miniature bottles of Scotch through the curtain partition.

In dealing with our client, I found myself tiptoeing through discussions and sugarcoating our conversations with conciliatory language. Bert, one of the principals in the firm we were representing, complained that Parker wasn't returning his phone calls, something that didn't come as a surprise to me.

Eventually Bert asked to start preparing for his deposition. Parker was supposed to have informed him that I would be handling the deposition, but he apparently hadn't. I became the communications pipeline between the client and its principal attorney.

Soon enough the clients got angry that their matter didn't seem to be getting any attention from the lawyer who was supposed to be in charge of their case.

After months of patience Bert exploded into a diatribe about how the lawyer he had hired was virtually incommunicado and ranted about being prepared by a lawyer a few decades his junior. He insisted on my giving him the name of Parker's hotel and the name of the judge he was appearing before out West.

Then strangely, Bert, himself a lawyer by training, complimented me on the way I was handling the case and apologized. He reminisced about his days as a first-year associate when he had found himself in a similar situation. I was relieved that he was satisfied with my work but sensed I hadn't assuaged his anger.

Soon after my conversation with Bert, the roof caved in on us. On the eve of the trial, I received a call from opposing counsel to inform me that Bert had contacted the plaintiffs and settled the case behind the lawyers' backs. Our client had agreed to pay the amount he had been sued for and legal fees for both sides—an amount that came to several hundred thousand dollars.

Parker had a public relations problem; it's rare—indeed, unheard of—for a client to settle a case without consulting with his or her attorney beforehand. And of course it's usually the lawyer who negotiates any settlement.

The realization that nine months of effort was for naught washed over me. I'd forgone weekends, parties, family, and everything else that makes such grinding work bearable. While Parker was busy trying to look good, a big one had gotten away. All the firm and I had to show for our efforts was egg splattered all over our faces.

I never worked with Parker again. To be honest, I never really spoke with him again. When he was in the office, he'd stride purposefully past my office, never pausing to exchange pleasantries or even glance in my direction. Apparently the disgrace of the case was such that it became necessary to have me ostracized. The rumor circulating among the partners was that I had carelessly allowed the attorney-client relationship to sour. It was as if I had become an untouchable. I believe I was made the fall guy.

But I came away from that experience a lot wiser than before. Ever since, I've never shied away from asking for guidance from someone more experienced if I needed it. Even more than I needed advice preparing the real estate case, I needed direction from someone on how to deal with Parker. It might not be easy to find such a mentor and it may be hard to trust others at first, but you've got to have allies in certain situations.

And of course, like any novice, I'm sure part of the neglect was the firm trying to put me to the test. My test just seemed a little more backbreaking than the ones most of my law school classmates had to face. I wasn't offended by Parker's brush-off. I understood the pressures he was under to maintain appearances. I felt I had succeeded in whatever he had thrown at me, and that gave me the ability to hold my head high. In the end, I provided a good service, although I think a little more direction would have made this junior associate a more effective advocate.

Having someone take a special interest in your

welfare not only gives you a person to discuss legal puzzles with but also someone to discuss the human side of dealing with the law.

Gregory D. Winfree, a graduate of Georgetown University Law School, is an in-house lawyer for a large corporation in Connecticut. He has been a lawyer for five years and aspires to establish his own sports apparel company.

15

My First Judicial Conference

William Dillof

I remember leaving home for the conference that morning feeling very impressed with myself in my cordovans and my spanking new Brooks Brothers suit. This was no ordinary day. Indeed, this was to be my first audience with none other than the rude and crude Judge T., a jurist renowned for his love of power and his willingness to exercise it. He was a man who delighted in dealing with artful slight to those who appeared before him.

A recent graduate of the University of Wisconsin Law School, I was a native New Yorker eager to test my mettle before the best the big city had to offer. Young but green, I was excited about my first chance to face down an adversary in a courtroom. I knew the meeting wasn't going to be a party; Judge T.'s reputation preceded him.

Nothing prepared me for the bizarre, almost surreal lack of decorum that characterized this particular Bronx courtroom of the early 1970s. Before the day was over I would experience that one-time-only kind of impotence and humiliation that it seems all novices experience early in their careers. It would also be my initiation into the dog-eat-dog world that is the setting for my legal career.

These days, the drive to the South Bronx from suburban Nassau County is dreary but routine. But on that day, about twenty years ago, the fact that I wasn't familiar with the route added one more thing for me to worry about. I absentmindedly mumbled the directions I clutched in my hands while I negotiated the thick early morning traffic. Crossing the Throgs Neck Bridge soon put me in a seedy section of the Big Apple, where I got on the Grand Concourse and drove for the first time into the dilapidated, unfamiliar territory of the South Bronx.

The neighborhood was low-slung and gray. Intimidating. I felt I was far away—indeed a world away—from the comfortable milieu of suburban Long Island. The streets were lined with rundown coffee shops, bodegas, and bargain stores. An occasional splash of yellow or orange cracked the colorless monotony of the scene.

I turned into the courthouse's dirt parking lot that seemed more an excavation site or a degrassed inner-city ball field. One edge of the lot was littered with construction equipment that looked as if it had no other place to call home while the two others were bordered by elevated railways whose traffic clattered and thundered above.

The courthouse sat like a huge mausoleum in a field of weeds. Beyond the rickety elevated train and through the thick, polluted air loomed Yankee Stadium, the area's most famous structure. To this day, I recall being struck by the incredible incongruity of the venerable courthouse and stadium amidst an endless plain of urban squalor. What I saw that first day inside the courthouse, too, seemed incongruous with a legal process that young lawyers, indeed nonlawyers, are taught to hold in such high esteem.

Following the advice of my boss, I entered the courthouse via a side entrance to avoid the crush of humanity that he said would greet me at the packed front entrance. I don't think it did much good, for I was immediately thrust into a world of staccato grunts, screams, cries, yells, and sobs. Crying babies and a variety of humanity in distress seemed to erupt from the ground like undergrowth in a forest, and I found myself dodging a phalanx of people to make my way a few dozen feet. A little discombobulated by the riotous ambience, I laboriously threaded my way into the elevator. I exited at the fourth floor and proceeded along a poorly lit corridor with pale green walls. As I rounded a corner, I nearly collided with two guards leading a young man in handcuffs.

I certainly am in good company, I thought to myself as I drew up in front of Judge T.'s courtroom. Well, here goes. . . .

The courtroom, which on conference days

served as the judge's outer chamber, was half the size of a school gym and its goings-on at least as fast paced as a game of ice hockey, it seemed. Its wood-paneled walls lent it a shabby dignity, and a tall warehouse window offered a vague access to the outside world. An ancient clock appeared to have fused itself into the wall on which it hung, and its hands had frozen at six-thirty who knows how long ago. Cold, hard light permeated the room through the sole window, which was a good thing, because half the light bulbs had burned out.

All around me murmured a hubbub of voices. Amid the vast sea of voices and faces, lawyers stood about in small clusters, confiding in low tones or laughing and shouting in loud voices. This unofficial banter I have come to know as the "currency of the marketplace." Here in this informal setting, my colleagues swapped war stories of their legal successes and defeats and here the fate of a client could be informally resolved or an unofficial settlement worked out. The whole thing brought to mind an unruly cattle auction. I was bewildered and overwhelmed as I approached a fading desk and signed in.

"Siddown, counselah, we'll call yuh when weeuh ready," came the receptionist's greeting, rendered in impeccable Bronxese.

I expected I'd be in and out in no more than an hour, but two hours later it was lunchtime and I felt as if I were hanging out in a doctor's office, waiting forever for "the doctor will see you now." The courtroom gradually quieted down as cases were called and heard.

Finally my case was called. I meekly entered the back room, where the judges conducted conferences. And it was a daunting room indeed, a smoke-filled back room worthy of the mythology of politics. Cigar smoke wafted about Judge T.'s chambers, which contained battered, unmatching furniture. Against the back wall, where one might have expected to see a picture of the scales of justice or a paean to God, ancient stick-on letters spelled out "Settle or Pick." A jury, that is. As in so many rooms, it seemed, a single window looked out sorrowfully on gritty streets.

A couple of lawyers, clerks, and secretaries scurried about and a guard stood still and watchful. Somewhere a telephone rang insistently, as if it, too, were in the hunt for attention in the chaotic atmosphere. It was just a more intimate rendering of everything I had seen in the courtroom and the hallway.

Into the room from an unassuming rear door slipped Larry W., a lawyer with a big Bronx practice and unsavory reputation. He wore short sleeves and sported a rich tan. To my amazement, Larry W., who had no connection with my case and shouldn't have been privy to the discussion that was about to take place, spread his lunch out on the empty corner of a desk and leisurely began to eat.

I thought I had gotten used to the craziness that had encased me that day—almost—but nothing prepared me for the audacity of this lawyer who, with no connection to this case, had turned the judge's chambers into his private cafeteria. Looking back, he didn't seem so out of place in the circus atmosphere that prevailed.

Where the smoke was thickest, behind a small desk by the lone window, hardly noticeable at first, sat my date with destiny. A diminutive man was the judge. He had a bird's small, gray eyes and he wore a tweed jacket that seemed more professorial than judicial. I guess I had fantasized that he would be sitting regally in his robes. From his mouth jutted a cigar the size of a Yankee souvenir baseball bat.

Because Larry W. had procured for himself the last free chair in the room, I remained standing, unsure what to expect. He continued to savor his lunch. And though he seemed indifferent to my presence, I guessed he was secretly reveling in my initiation before his friend, the judge.

Further preliminaries were had and the briefing began. My adversary, Bob Landers, a debonair lawyer from the city comptroller's office, made his introduction and then the judge gave me what I assumed would be his undivided attention.

"What do you want?" he shot at me. His voice was unforgettable: a cool nasal tone of voice that boomed with smug authority. It was then that I knew that I was in the presence of the great Judge T.

"What we have, Your Honor," I began, "is the case of a young woman who, during childbirth three years ago, was given a fourth-degree laceration of the perineum as a result—" I stopped cold. I noticed he wasn't paying attention to me or what I was saying.

Judge T. had turned around to speak with his secretary. I also had lost the attention of Bob Landers, who seemed to be daydreaming out the window. Larry W., still eating his eternal sandwich, was arguing vociferously on the phone with someone he addressed as Maureen, between gulps. If she could understand what he was saying through the muffled pronunciation of a full mouth, she was to be commended. The judge's assistants came and went through the rear door. I realized no one really gave a hoot about my client's perineum.

After some time, Judge T. swung around, peered straight into my eyes, and softly addressed my adversary. "Why don't you tell me about this one, Bob," he said. Landers's eyes never budged from their gaze out the window. He said simply and dryly, "It was repaired."

Larry W. got off the phone, and everyone in the room followed the judge's lead and focused their attention on my response.

"Your Honor," I said with as much swagger as I could muster, "this was a young woman. The injury and the repair have left her with a great deal of pain during intimate relations with her husband."

Removing his cigar from his mouth, Judge T. tapped off the ash directly onto his stained and tattered desk blotter. He peered over each shoulder, seemingly to assure himself he had an audience, and curled his mouth into a hard "is this kid for real?" half-smile.

"It's supposed to hoit!" he explained in a Bowery Boys accent. The room filled with conspiratorial laughter. Refusing to relinquish my young dignity, I laughed along, too, but not as loudly. I had my pride. Finally, the judge, who had not himself laughed, asked me what my "demand" was. What he meant was how much did my client want to settle the case.

The amount I proposed provoked still more disdainful laughter from Landers, and appeared to prompt Judge T. to call his next case while he impaled me with those feral eyes. It was only later that I learned that I was putting on the table twice as much as my client could expect to receive.

"Mr. Dillof," said Judge T., pointing his cigar accusingly at me, "don't come back until you're prepared to talk."

Had I only known then that this incident was Judge T.'s typical way of dealing with my office's lawyers I would not have felt so dejected as I did then, trudging out again into the Bronx streets. Other judges I encountered that first year had their personal quirks. But I can't remember one who was all at once less attentive, had a less wide-ranging knowledge of the law, and carried on proceedings in such a chaotic atmosphere. Exposure to that court-room's eccentricities wasn't the only remembrance I took away with me. Today, I also recall one of my first glimpses of a world of tragedy and affliction, a world that lawyers, in their privileged position in society, usually don't experience firsthand.

Looking back on that event, I'm confident that it was not my tender age or my fancy Ivy League clothes that moved the judge to humiliate me so. Indeed, I appeared before Judge T. many times after that, and was always accorded the same degree of respect.

William Dillof, a New York City personal injury lawyer specializing in medical malpractice, practices law at the same firm he went to work for fresh out of law school at the University of Wisconsin twenty years ago.

they stepped up to it. But I can't remember one who was as articulate [illegible] had a less [illegible] knowledge of the law, and created in proceedings [illegible] such a [illegible] atmosphere [illegible] to the courtroom [illegible] the only remembrance I took away with me. Today I also [illegible] one of [illegible] glimpse of a world of tragedy and affliction, a world that [illegible] privileged position in society, usually don't experience firsthand.

Looking back on the event, I'm confident that it was not [illegible] my [illegible] that [illegible] the judge [illegible] I appeared before Judge [illegible] many times after that, and was always accorded the same degree of respect.

William [illegible] New York City [illegible] [illegible] [illegible] [illegible] University of [illegible] [illegible]

16

Booty in the Law Library

Darien McWhirter

They were as big as linebackers, those casually dressed men with their strangely street-smart attitudes striding through our button-down law office. As my eyes followed the muscular 250-pound frames into Bill's office, I thought these were two men I wouldn't want to encounter in a dark alley. Bill, like me an associate in the firm, closed his office door. I returned to my work, a bit distracted and curious.

Later, when Bill showed these behemoths to the door, I could see my colleague was shaken. His mood was anxious and his skin pale. He scanned the floor like a bird nervously pecking at the ground. He looked over at me. He seemed about to start telling me something important. But the voice of the secretary intervened, announcing his next appointment. Bill turned to address his client. I went home, still curious.

Early the next morning I pulled out a legal volume in the firm's law library, heard a jangling sound, and onto the floor fell a spaghetti-thin gold necklace. What was this, hidden treasure? And what was it doing stashed in the law library? My first thought was that someone was using the necklace as a bookmark. I peered into the space where the book had been and saw several more neck-laces. Before I had a chance to ponder the plausibility of my conclusion, Fred, the firm's profane but paternal partner, was in the doorway, staring at me and my booty.

"Look," I said, "isn't this funny? I just found these necklaces!"

Fred wasn't amused. He probably assumed the cache of gold was mine, but before I had a chance to clear my good name, in walked Mary, another associate. Like me, Mary denied any knowledge of the necklaces.

As we stood there discussing the possibilities, Bill entered the office, looking sheepish and, I thought, more than a bit guilty.

Bill saw Fred holding the necklaces and his face turned red. Fred hastily called a closed-door meeting. Strict instructions were given to the secretary: "No calls, no interruptions."

Sitting behind an expansive, engraved desk, Fred held court. "Okay, what's the story on this?" he asked, fixing his eyes on Bill. Bill gulped an audible breath.

"Well, it's like this," he began. "Two clients came in yesterday for legal advice. They had taken some jewelry from a jewelry store the day before and they were having second thoughts about the life of crime they had embarked upon. They were also afraid the police were hot on their trail and they wanted to know what to do with the evidence."

"And what did you tell them?" Fred asked calmly. He closed his eyes, as he often did, and appeared to be soaking up every word with his whole body. Fred had seen it all. He once told us of visiting a client at his home to find the guy ironing money that he used to pay Fred. Fred figured the guy dug the money up from his backyard, washed it, and then apparently decided it needed a good pressing. Talk about laundering money.

Bill continued. "All I could think of was that they might leave our office and be arrested right at the front door. I didn't think that was a good idea for them—or us—so I told them to give me the jewelry." Silence.

"And then?" Fred asked. He opened his eyes.

"And then I had to do something with it, so I hid it in the law books in the law library," Bill confessed.

The first thing that ran through my mind was that law school certainly hadn't prepared me for this quandary. I searched my memory trying to decide what Perry Mason would have done in a situation like this, but no brilliant ideas came to me. On the one hand I knew lawyers have no business receiving stolen goods or withholding evidence. On the other hand, a lawyer's first duty is to the client, and a lawyer should avoid doing anything that might jeopardize the client's case.

Fred asked for our views on how the matter should be handled.

This was going to be interesting, unlike much of what I did at the firm during my first year practicing law at this small-town, eastern Texas law firm. The first few weeks I learned what it means to practice general law. I handled real estate transactions, divorces, criminal cases, and disputes of every kind. This meant I never had time to become a true expert in any particular area of the law. I showed up in court at the appointed time as prepared as the press of the other cases would allow. During my busiest weeks, I would be juggling three dozen matters while Fred and the other more senior associates worked fewer but more important and challenging cases.

I learned that whereas law school teaches you about law, it does not get you ready to face the day-to-day problems of practicing law. My best teachers were the lawyers around me who taught me the stuff that wasn't in the law books. I began to ask them to eat lunch with me so that I could pick their brains. Most of what I know about how to really practice law I learned that first year during my lunch hours.

This was information that won cases, even though it couldn't be considered remotely legal. One judge regularly left for a four o'clock date on the golf links. If your client had a weak case, they taught, make sure you get a late hearing before this judge so he doesn't have time to make a carefully considered ruling. Then there were the "hanging judges," the ones who always imposed the maximum penalty allowable. Got a weak case before a hanging judge? Settle the case with the prosecutor to make sure the judge doesn't have the chance to throw the book at your client. If your case gets assigned to a defendant-friendly judge, take a chance on a trial. That kind of stuff. The stuff they *can't* teach in the classroom.

Then there was the infamous bloodstain on the lawyer's second-floor office. This elderly sole practitioner delighted in telling me how in a divorce case he was handling, the father of his client's opponent showed up in the lawyer's office one day and shot him! Just like that. Lesson for the new lawyer: Family law and divorce cases are more dangerous than other fields of law.

Another thing that fascinated me during those first few weeks was the amount of information I soon came to know about a great many people in the community. It always amazed me how much that was really intriguing seemed to get past our local newspapers. Of course, I was obligated to keep all this juicy gossip to myself because telling others would violate the attorney-client privilege. That rule basically says that everything a lawyer knows about his or her client is a secret unless the client gives permission to reveal it or reveals the information to a third party him- or herself.

Our linebacker types were entitled to that confidentiality. They had taken Bill into their confidence and we could not turn them in. However, holding the jewelry might expose us to criminal charges if we didn't handle the matter properly. Despite its comical side, this case had to be disposed of delicately.

Mary suggested that we turn over the jewelry to the police. The rest of us did not think that a very good idea. The police might be able to trace it back to our clients, and we would have violated our duty to protect the clients' interests. I suggested that we send the necklaces back to the jewelry store they had been stolen from in the first place. Fred rejected this idea as also potentially risky for our clients.

Fred turned to Bill and asked him what he thought we should do now that he had had some time to reflect on his actions. Bill, in a moment of true redemption, suggested giving the jewelry back to the clients. It was decided that this was the only course of action that would get the law firm out of the picture and put things back the way they were when Bill mistakenly accepted the jewelry.

Bill and I made sure all of the jewelry was out of the books in the library, and he called the two gentlemen and asked them to come back to the office. They arrived in less than an hour, but while waiting for them my imagination ran wild. Movie clips and TV images from the evening news raced through my head. I could see the police bursting into our office with guns drawn demanding the jewelry—jewelry that might have been worth a few hundred dollars at most. I had visions of the police arresting our linebackers as they left the office, and perhaps hauling us lawyers off for questioning as well. Images of Lieutenant Trag threatening Perry Mason with disbarment and jail for concealing evidence danced in my head.

When the two clients arrived, I showed them into Bill's office and closed the door. I then sat down next to Bill as he explained that we had discussed the matter and felt it would be better for them to take back the jewelry.

We recommended two alternative courses of action for them. They could turn themselves in with the jewelry. If they did that, they probably would ultimately be guilty of a felony, with fines and criminal records, but could be spared jail time to compensate them for their honesty. Their other option was to box up the jewelry and mail it back to the store where they had filched it. I'd seen nothing in the local newspapers about the heist. For all we knew, the store hadn't even missed the necklaces.

The two clients listened intently to everything Bill said and left with the jewelry. We never heard from them again and so assumed they either sent the jewelry back, sold it, or threw it down a storm drain.

Phew! We had dodged a bullet. But Bill's crisis made me reflect on that human propensity for anyone who has gained some knowledge to think they know it all. There are many times when lawyers have no choice but to shoot from the hip and hope for the best. However, in most instances, there is time to get a second opinion; run it by someone else, and see the reaction. This takes only a minute and can save everyone involved a lot of grief. That is what Bill should have done and that is what I learned to do more over time as my quick answers to legal questions led me into deep water on more than one occasion. Often I'd felt I owed a client a quick answer. After all, he or she was paying for my expertise. Bill had only thought about what might happen if his clients were arrested at our door. He had not thought through what we could do, legally and ethically, once we had possession of the property.

Some people might feel that it is terrible that these two men apparently did not pay for their crime. Viewed idealistically, that's probably true. However, most lawyers who deal with the criminal justice system no longer have the illusion that penitentiaries are places where criminals are reformed. In retrospect, if our clients were scared into giving up a life of crime and the state was spared the expense of prosecuting them and paying their prison room and board for a couple of years, everyone was probably better off.

I left that small firm after less than a year. The strain of trying to be prepared every Monday morning for a different kind of case was simply too much for me at the time. I decided to specialize in a particular area of the law and had to reduce the time spent in the courtroom. However, I'll never forget the lessons I learned trying to handle every legal problem that walked through the door during that first year.

Lawyers often refer to making a client whole, something I like to call putting Humpty Dumpty back together again. Usually that means money in return for injuries suffered or property wrongly taken. In this case, we were making our clients—and ourselves, I noted—whole by turning the clock back to before they stepped across the office threshold.

I'll never forget the way Fred handled this and other situations. Young lawyers make mistakes. Fred never yelled at us. He would twist up his face as if to say How could you do that? and then get right to the issue of fixing whatever we had done wrong. The reality is that everyone has to start somewhere, and the only way you learn is by doing—making mistakes, correcting them, and going on to the next case.

Or, as Fred put it so tastily: "Law is like baking a cake. No one cares how much flour you spill on the floor. They only care what the cake tastes like."

Darien McWhirter is a graduate of the University of Texas Law School. Now based in San Jose, California, he is a member of the California and Texas bar associations. He has written several books about the law.

17

When Law Became More Than Research

Monica Miller

Janet was good to the five or six people who worked under her. Once a month or so—before austerity was instituted—she treated her telecommunications law underlings to lunch. Although we met to discuss cases, the casual mealtime settings also helped strengthen ties among the close-knit members of her office clan. Janet possessed a bold personality and knew how to let her hair down. So when my mentor buzzed me on the phone and asked that I come upstairs to her office, I hurried up there. I've got an interesting project for us to work on, Janet said.

With the customary alacrity that unfailingly triggered curiosity in those who worked for her, Janet presented the following question: Would the federal government require our client, a small high-technology firm, to obtain a license before selling its new technology to the public?

I was a recent law school graduate who, like

most of my colleagues, spent many hours in the law library plodding diligently through textbooks and familiarizing myself with the finer points of rarefied legal arguments. I'd graduated as a walking law encyclopedia and was confident I'd usually find the answers using my research skills. For the first few months of my legal career, my stick-to-the-book strategy had worked well. I billed hours dutifully, applying the expensive technical wisdom accumulated during three years of law school. I assumed, despite Janet's warning that current regulations and precedent might not provide much guidance, that the context of this question would reveal an easy answer once I started digging.

I was an eager beaver, anxious to please, and plunged into a painstaking, all-bases-covered inquiry into our client's obligations. I had no doubt that by the end of my task, I'd be able to proclaim the rights of our client. It never seriously occurred to me that Washington, with its vast repositories of bureaucratic and regulatory enlightenment, would be silent on the subject.

Of course, Janet's hunch proved correct. Research from early afternoon until almost midnight and an exhaustive search on *Westlaw,* a computer database, turned up no helpful answer. Like many of my fellow associates, I also undertook several hours of research on my own time; I felt uneasy about billing a client for my inexperience.

Since I found nothing in my research that appeared to apply to what our client was proposing to do, I naively reported back to Janet that it appeared our client firm was free to do as it pleased. End of case. However, as I was to discover, legal research can be just the beginning of a lawyer's duty to a client.

Janet told me I had assumed too much. She then explained that just because a federal agency hadn't promulgated a regulation governing this new technology, it didn't necessarily mean that the agency would refrain from regulating our client's service if it found it out in the marketplace. Our work was just beginning, she said.

Indeed, my research was the first step in what would become a case that at times took on some semblance of a Madison Avenue public relations campaign. In effect, we became marketers of our client's service, selling the concept rather than the product itself to regulators. Eventually, we would promote our client's service at the highest levels of a federal agency. Our campaign would seek simultaneously to explain the benefits of our client's service and to convince the authorities that it should be provided for in the regulatory scheme, even though there was nothing there in the first place. Our mission was to preempt regulation by creating our own.

Step by step, Janet walked me through the process of presenting our client to the agency in the best way possible. We first had to determine the type of license the agency might require. We then tried to anticipate what kind of license regulators might require of users of the service as well. The idea was to construct a regulation that would mesh the two. As it turned out, the agency would require only our client to obtain a license for the technology.

Janet's insistence that I begin an assignment with as much insight as possible was typical of her approach. In contrast to some partners, who could be condescending and intolerant regardless of their sex, Janet was patient and helpful. She was stingy neither with her time nor her infectious personality. Janet didn't waste her experience but whenever possible directed me to sources she knew would make my life easier. My lawyer friends often told me of stories in which they were expected to track down obscure cases without partners' providing guidance. They were told to bill their learning time to the client.

Moreover, as a successful woman partner, Janet was very much a role model for me in a profession that remains overwhelmingly male. Janet fetched her own coffee and offered to bring you some as well. Yet, as any good boss does, she always made it clear who was in charge.

As we bored in on the issues in the case, we realized that agencies other than the applicable agency might be interested in the service and might assist our efforts in minimizing the bureaucratic hassle we feared.

Much of the next few months I spent wading through Washington's byzantine bureaucracy. It was exceedingly difficult to get our nose in the door, and I became frustrated with unreturned phone calls. Not only did we have to contend with the usual frustration of dealing with overworked bureaucrats but also, ironically, we were not a high-priority issue because there was at the time nothing on the books about what we were doing. Part of my job was to identify State Department personnel who might show an interest in our client firm's technology. Another facet of our strategy was to emphasize that a neighboring government already had approved the technology for use within its borders. We would save that fact for our face-to-face meeting with our agency contact.

Finally, months of preparation materialized as a colorful booklet replete with diagrams outlining the system with pictures of trucks and satellites linked by arrows and lines. We provided background on our client's product line and goals and detailed the benefits of the service. A bulleted question-and-answer section responded to questions we thought would be posed. An impressive piece of work, it was intended to influence with its appearance as much as its content.

Most of the information in the booklet was provided by the client, and almost all of the production was done by people working with the firm's new in-house desktop publishing capabilities. I can't take much credit for its polished look; my role in assembling our masterpiece consisted of little more than collating the pages and reading the final version for clarity.

After the booklet had been perfected, we began preparing for our meeting with the representative from the agency. Janet and I held mock interviews at which we tried to anticipate and answer questions that might be thrown at us. These weeks of preparation required relatively little legal research into case law and precedent but, on the other hand, demanded a whole lot of creativity. We tried to put ourselves in the regulator's shoes. Several months later, booklet in hand and preparations complete, we were ready to take our client's case to the agency.

The whole idea of presenting our case to a warm body at first seemed blasphemous to me. To try to influence a federal agency's decision initially seemed tantamount to asking the United States Supreme Court to divulge how it would rule on any controversial issue you might name. After watching and listening to partners call up agency members to ask questions, I realized this is the way business is done. Once we greeted a commissioner on the street and discussed a point in the case. The executive branch of government, at least with regulatory matters, didn't have any of the secrecy and aura that the judiciary did. So our handsome booklet did serve a purpose. Janet ended up doing most of the talking at the hour-long meeting, but I learned a valuable lesson—that research skills can provide information for decision making far beyond a courtroom.

Ultimately our client proceeded with the tracking

system and has earned many American and Canadian dollars for the project. The lesson I learned, and thoroughly enjoyed learning, was that not all the answers to legal questions are found in the rules, regulations, and cases. When working in Washington, it is not uncommon to pick up the yellow telephone directory of federal agencies and dial bureaucrats directly, and sometimes the best sources of information are people working at the regulating agency itself. Not only might they answer your question and save you considerable time and your client considerable money but you also may have greater confidence that you have the correct answer. Of course it does not hurt to verify the information by checking the standard legal sources. By phrasing the question in the correct manner, you might win a bureaucrat to your side, further simplifying the task of achieving your goal. One of the key things I learned that first year was how to ask questions . . . and what questions to ask . . . and whom to ask.

Finally, I learned that the regulator need not be the adversary and can be your ally if included in your plans. A little courtesy goes a long way.

Monica Miller has been practicing law for five years. She works as a clerk for a federal judge in Southern California.

18

Liberated from the Law

Noreen Marcus

I left the practice of law after six months. But even though more than seven years have passed since then, I still do not regret becoming a lawyer. Practicing law during the months leading up to my father's death made him very proud of his daughter and only child. Just as I owe much of the course of my legal career to my father, so do I owe its brevity and abrupt end to his death. In retrospect, my decision to become a lawyer is as responsible for what I am today as for what I'm not.

A journalist before going to law school, I found that practicing law inexorably drove me back to the work that I had originally loved and ultimately matched me with an employer who could offer me work I found fulfilling: editing a daily newspaper that specializes in covering lawyers and the law. For me, the law served as a tool that opened up journalistic avenues that I might never have had access to otherwise. Most important, perhaps, my experience during that first year forced me to confront what I really did want to do with my life. I learned that although I didn't want to practice law, I could use journalism to write about it.

I'll always be glad I was inducted into the Illinois bar if for no other reason than that my father got to attend my swearing-in ceremony. It was a highlight of his life.

In 1984, newly divorced and with my J.D. in hand, I moved back to Chicago, my hometown, from Miami. I hadn't lived in Chicago for ten years, but I'd always been exceptionally close to my father. He raised me from the age of thirteen, when my mother died. When I returned, he was recently retired after forty-five years as a postal clerk and in the throes of ending an unhappy second marriage. I was moving back to Illinois in part because I thought he needed me, and it seemed like a good time to try to sever my ties with Miami and try a change of scene.

I arrived in Chicago with a distinct professional disadvantage. The Windy City has six law schools turning out fresh-faced graduates every year. In addition, to an employer in Illinois, "UM" means the nearby, first-rate University of Michigan, not the University of Miami School of Law, from which I had graduated. I wasn't on the law review or at the top of my class (actually, I had just made it into the top third). I did manage to get some low-paid research work at a downtown Chicago firm that had a piece of a massive asbestos property damage case, but the lead partner was a stuffy Ivy Leaguer who didn't treat me with the respect I thought my age, thirty-three, and background deserved and I was happy when the job ended. During that prebar-examination time, I perused the newspaper ads and found work on a writing project for the office of the special counsel of the United Auto Workers. As ever, I was being paid to write, and this time it was a section of an internal report the office was preparing. That was a happier experience because the special counsel recognized that I could do what none of his crack lawyer-investigators could do: write.

My father supported me financially and emotionally. He grew up during the Great Depression and had only a high school diploma. He wanted better for me and he always encouraged me in everything I set out to do. His support while I studied for the bar was just more of the same. This, and his deep-felt pride, had the natural effect of making me want to succeed for him as well as for myself.

Wouldn't you want to do well for someone, who, while delivering meals to shut-ins (one of his retirement hobbies), would drop an extra one off for you so you wouldn't have to put aside your study guides to cook?

People of all kinds were drawn to my father. His network of friends led to a surprising step in my career. When he finally left his second wife, he moved into the back room of a house of a woman who took in boarders in the Chicago suburb of Skokie. There he met another roomer named Maria, a big, gregarious Mexican woman, a community activist. She and my father became fast friends. Naturally he told her all about his daughter who had just passed the bar exam and was looking for work.

Maria told him about a little downtown firm that did the considerable immigration work she sent their way. She spoke with them, and pretty soon they were welcoming me into their fold and giving me piecework—uncontested divorces, corporate papers, real estate closings, simple immigration matters. By taking a modest hourly sum, I helped with overhead, including the salary of a secretary whose daily hour spent watching her favorite soap was sacrosanct.

I think I liked them because they weren't your stereotypical button-down, humorless, rigid attorney types. They were laid-back, a tad skeptical of authority. They reminded me of journalists.

Pat and her father worked there. Lively, Irish Pat was an aspiring playwright and a former Equal Employment Opportunity Commission lawyer who obviously relished the discrimination cases that came her way. I'll never forget the bright gold wool blazer she once wore to the office—just the kind of thing that would have scandalized my tutorial instructor in law school.

John, the other beginning lawyer attached to this loose confederation, dated a clothes designer and was part of an artsy crowd. Warren, the lead partner, adhered to his family's tradition of following the horses (I never did understand exactly what that meant) between bouts of legal work.

So I enjoyed my colleagues, if not my vocation. The work was monotonous, soul-numbing stuff. Immigration work at that level is a matter of waiting in crowded rooms and filling out lots of forms. Even simple divorces, which require much patience and empathy, were something I found draining and unsatisfying. The more complicated immigration matters never seemed to end. There never seemed to be a sense of closure or a benchmark of genuine progress. It was so unlike newspaper journalism, where you'd take home the product of your labors at the end of every day.

Moreover, I found preparing pro forma legal documents stymied my creative impulses. In short, I needed a professional outlet to express myself, and the practice of law wasn't providing that outlet. Before going to law school in Miami, I had worked for seven years as a copy editor at several newspapers, most recently at the *Miami News*, which has since folded. I missed it but was loath to disappoint my father, who was so proud of me and my budding legal career.

I started dreaming about returning to Miami and to journalism, and after several months got the courage to broach the subject with my father. He urged me to keep at law, saying that once I got through this apprenticeship I would have a fine career. So I kept at it.

Then suddenly he died. It was his heart, and his death was completely unexpected. He had no warnings, no symptoms, and had worked his usual meal route on December 31. He collapsed on New Year's Day, 1986, stayed alive for a day—just long enough to see the people he loved—and then expired. I was devastated, and as was my habit at times of deep sorrow, turned to writing for immediate solace. All through the night of January 2, I sat up writing his eulogy. As my cousin delivered it in my name at the funeral, one of the lawyers I worked with turned to a relative and said, "She's so talented." A good writer, they said. "Why is she practicing law?"

Why, indeed. Without my father to cheer me on, I'd lost my impetus to keep going. Putting together the eulogy had reminded me how important the act of writing is to me.

For about a month I moved around in a daze, dealing mostly with getting my father's affairs in order. The lawyers I worked with were wonderful. They let me hang out at the office, not doing very much. It was just a comfortable place to be.

For the first time in my life, I was absolutely free, beholden to no one. I could do exactly what I wanted, so what did I want to do?

That month I got wind through the journalists' grapevine that Steve Brill, editor of *American Lawyer* magazine, had bought the *Review* newspapers in south Florida, specialty dailies covering law, business, and real estate. I respected Brill, who like me was a law school graduate with a penchant for journalism. Brill had introduced a hard edge into the coverage of legal journalism, covering lawyers as they are, challenging their self-image as professionals who rarely or never soil their souls by thinking about money. Instead of delving solely into the finer points of legal precedent, Brill emphasized the study of law as a business.

An old colleague from the *Miami News* was running the *Miami Review*. I called him and a month later I was in Miami spending a week on a tryout as a copy editor.

Not long after that, a cousin of mine in Chicago called me. I was surprised to hear from him. He offered to get me an interview at the old-line law firm where he worked. Before my father's death, the cousin had told me that a nepotism policy stood in the way of my working at his firm. Since I considered this particular member of the family tree a parochial snob who believes that Florida lawyers get their training in the Everglades between periods of 'gator wrestling, I thought there might be other forces at work. I suspected that because he liked my father, the cousin probably felt a little guilty about having earlier brushed me off. But the lure of journalism was too strong, and I didn't pursue the opportunity. By this time, I was happy to inform him that I'd already taken a job as a copy editor at the *Miami Review*.

Noreen Marcus is executive editor of The Palm Beach Daily Business Review, *a daily newspaper of business, law, and real estate in West Palm Beach, Florida.*

Index